Quest
for the Virgins

Book Three
of the
Quest Series

David Beaupré

Published by buddha bees

cover design and graphics by David Beaupré
cover photo by Steven Heap

Quest for the Virgins
© 2015 David Beaupré

Published by buddha bees

"With a unique perspective for the almost unnoticed, 'Quest for the Virgins' will deliver a less common experience of a most popular place."

The Quest Series
by David Beaupré

Quest and Crew
Quest on the Thorny Path
Quest for the Virgins
Quest in the Caribbean

Quest for the Virgins is a work of non-fiction. All places, characters, and events are real. In some cases the names of characters have been altered.

ISBN-13: 978-0692371633   **buddha bees**

ISBN-10: 069237163X

Introduction to Quest for the Virgins

Find our crew poised and ready to venture into the dreaded Mona Passage between Hispaniola and Puerto Rico. We're on our way for a long, leisurely sail on the beautiful south coast of Puerto Rico. It is my pleasure to have you come along for the third book in the Quest series. Included in the itinerary is Vieques, St. Croix, St. John and a little Virgin Gorda. With a unique perspective for the almost unnoticed, 'Quest for the Virgins' will deliver a less common experience of a most popular place. Be whisked away to warm tropical destinations for a humorous glimpse into the life aboard a sailboat in the Caribbean.

Introduction to The Quest Series

My wife and I are very fortunate to have followed a path in life that brings us closer to our dreams and to each other. It's nice work when you can get it. From the day we met, our lives have been filled with extraordinary experiences. Somewhere in a lifetime of memorable adventures we purchased a classic sailboat. Little did we guess the implications of preparing Quest and her crew for a life on the ocean. Learning our lessons along the way, Wendy and I were slowly transformed into sailors. From launching Quest in north Florida to a Category 5 hurricane in Grenada, we discover that the art of living on a sailboat is much more than rum-infused beach parties. It was hard work to have fun. But when all the chores are done and the storms have passed, Wendy and I consider ourselves fortunate to have fulfilled our dreams. Everyone can learn to be the master of their destiny. If time does not permit you to sail the ocean blue, I offer you this four book series on how two friends found happiness in their personal quest for paradise. The Quest Series is a true modern sailing story. Come along, let's take this extraordinary journey together.

Introduction to Quest and Crew

How many people have dreamed about sailing away and leaving it all behind? Here's how it happened. 'Quest and Crew' is the first book of a four book series. The story begins hours before a devastating Category 5 hurricane obliterates the south shore of Grenada. It's a story about the many twists and turns that life can take. The sailboat Quest gained a new lease on life with a complete retrofit in the backwoods of North Carolina. The job of the crew becoming real sailors began in North Palm Beach. On a clear starry night, we left South Florida on a hope enveloped by a dream. Finding ourselves at the beginning of a new adventure, we set sail and anchored one island at a time through the Bahamas. The Caribbean is a few books away. Here is a glimpse into the powerful attraction of sailboats and sapphire water. 'Quest and Crew' is all about the joy of success as well as what it takes to overcome the occasional disaster. From beginning to end, the book is about transforming a rookie crew and beautiful old boat into a sailing adventure. Come for the hurricane, stay for the story.

Introduction to Quest on the Thorny Path

Not all trips to paradise are smooth sailing. 'Quest on the Thorny Path' is the second book of the Quest series. Leave the laid back cruiser hangout of Georgetown, Bahamas behind and hit the big ocean waves for the first time. From Georgetown we take the path less traveled through the deserted out islands of the Bahamas. After a short stay in the Turks and Caicos we follow a route along the north coast of Hispaniola that Christopher Columbus appropriately named the 'Thorny Path'. The book is a true adventure about overcoming fear and dangerous challenges in one of sailing's harshest proving grounds. Bashing through heavy seas and strong headwinds on a lee shore isn't for everyone. But at least you can read about it.

Introduction to Quest in the Caribbean

The final book in the Quest series is 'Quest in the Caribbean'. Wendy and I have become full time sailors. The sea has been kind to us. It has been our home, a very strict master and unforgiving teacher. We slowly learned our lessons of seamanship one day at a time. But more importantly we learned a great deal about each other and what it takes to be good companions on a tiny boat. 'Quest for the Caribbean' begins on a beautiful day in the British Virgin Islands. When we pass through the dangerous, narrow, reef-strewn passage in Virgin Gorda and enter the Caribbean we are just one boat length closer to fulfilling our dream. There are many more islands to explore and miles to sail before the journey is complete. Some of the wonders that await our eager eyes are Saba, the fabled 'island in the clouds' and the neighboring island of Statia. The serenely beautiful island of Nevis, Montserrat's volcanoes, the gentle people of Dominica, Saint Lucia and the Grenadines all enrich our lives. 'Quest for the Caribbean' ends on the south shore of Grenada as we are about to fulfill a destiny that was many hard years in the making.

David Beaupré
Fall River, Tennessee

Contents

One

Under the Radar

The eighty mile strait between the eastern tip of Hispaniola and Puerto Rico is a turbulent and dangerous body of water. It is a proving ground and a watery grave for many. The natural events that combine to make the Mona Passage a subject of folklore are varied and complex. It is a place where ferocious currents are exchanged between the Atlantic Ocean and the Caribbean Sea over meandering shallows. The shifting sand of the shallows constantly alters the direction and intensity of the currents. At the northern end of the Mona Passage, the Puerto Rican trench drops six miles straight down to the bottom of the ocean. This causes the warm water of the Caribbean to mingle with the cold water of the PR trench creating surface turbulence that is as reliable as 'Old Faithful'.

If the dangerous currents and a very bumpy sea are not sufficient to get a boater's attention, there is an atmospheric condition that will. On most days, huge stormcells are generated over the island of Puerto Rico by a fierce tropical sun. As the sun sets, the storm cells are forced off the western coast of PR by the trade winds. By midnight, the storms build into monster cells which produce squall line after squall line. In summary, crossing the Mona from Hispaniola to Puerto Rico is marked by extreme headwinds, aggressive shifting currents, patches of water with sufficient turbulence to toss a small sailboat around like flotsam, and ends with storm squalls capable of capsizing small craft. That is on a good day. On a very bad day, boats and crews are lost without a trace.

On the morning of our sail across the Mona, Quest lay at anchor in the roadstead of Playa Macao at the eastern tip of Hispaniola. We had one short hour before sunrise. I had one very thoughtful hour to consider the fateful consequences of crossing the dreaded Mona Passage. I inspected the rigging and checked the lashing on the dinghy. Raw emotion distracted an otherwise logical process. My thoughts strayed to an interesting conversation which Wendy and I had with the owner of a boat chandlery in Samana the previous week. Wendy and I had been strolling down a back alley in the beautiful city of Samana in the Dominican Republic when we found ourselves seeking shelter from a passing shower. We ran to the nearest shop awning. I looked through a small grimy window into a poorly lighted shop.

"Take a look at this" I said.

There were hundreds of outboard engines.

"It looks like a pawn shop" Wendy replied.

Every description of outboard was proudly displayed on sawhorses in various states of misuse. I opened the door and gestured to Wendy.

"No, you first" she said.

A dark middle aged gentleman with the casual air of a used car dealer strolled nonchalantly to my side.

"Let me guess. You are perhaps looking for your dinghy engine?" he said.

Wendy and I looked at each other in surprise. He looked back even more surprised.

"The Guardia didn't send you?" he asked sheepishly.

The rain shower had led Wendy and me to inadvertently walk through the door of the Samana stolen outboard engine superstore.

"No sir; the police did not send me to buy an outboard" I said.

"Well then, it is always a good time to upgrade at Robados Outboards. It is still raining. Can I offer you a cup of coffee?" he said with a broad smile.

Wendy accepted his offer.

When he had disappeared into the back room to pour Wendy's coffee, I whispered "Let him talk."

The Duke of Dinghy Engines entered with a demitasse of strong coffee.

"So how does this trade up program work?" I asked.

"Boaters like you can trade their outboard for a bigger size. Everyone can use a little more size" he said throwing a poorly concealed wink in Wendy's direction.

"How about the 'local' trade up program?" I asked.

"There is a big need in Samana for 100 hp engines."

"Fishermen?" I asked.

"Some times" he winked.

I motioned with my hands for him to continue and said "Please tell me more."

"You know what goes on in the Mona?" he asked.

"I know a little" I said with a grin.

Actually I didn't have the slightest idea what he was talking about.

"It's very good business" he said.

Then he elaborated on his take on the clandestine trafficking in illegal immigration to Puerto Rico. Hispaniola is a very poor island with Haiti the poorer of the two countries that comprise Hispaniola. (Haiti remains the poorest country in the Americas and one of the poorest in the world according to the World Bank.) Puerto Rico is only 80 miles away from the poorest island in the Western Hemisphere. It is the 'Promised Land' compared to the squalid existence in the slums of Port-au-Prince. One thousand dollars is the going price to be whisked away from poverty and deposited on the shores of the United States of America.

The one thousand dollar fee to cross the Mona strait does not include luxury accouterments. It is a long ride on a wooden bench in an open boat. The normal sea state and weather conditions in the Mona Passage are dangerous in a well equipped vessel. Making the passage in a leaking wooden pirogue with a mercenary as a captain is Russian roulette. When the weather is particularly foul, the small craft doesn't stand a chance. Hundreds of crowded boats are lost each year. Put your thousand dollars down and spin the wheel.

Under the Radar

'Robados Outboards' did their level best to supply a steady output of clean 100 hp outboard engines for the benefit of the human traffickers. This side of his business did not directly affect the cruiser. The dinghy motors on cruising boats are smaller than 100 hp. Quest's dinghy was powered by a 5 hp Johnson. A five horsepower outboard is a glorified egg scrambler. It is not for ocean use. Although the selling of 100 hp engines did not have a direct effect on the cruiser, the ancillary trading in the outboard upgrade market by 'Robados Outboards' most certainly inconvenienced many cruisers. Many small outboard engines go missing from the stern of cruisers' boats in Samana. The local police advise cruisers to chain and lock their motors onto the transom of their dinghies. Robados also had a decent selection of industrial strength bolt cutters available for sale.

"The trade up plan is very simple" Señor Robados explained. "If you bring in two ten horse motors to trade you get a twenty horse. If someone brings in two twenty horse motors they take away a forty horse. Eventually they work up to 100 hp and they can start a small business."

"Do the police get involved?" I asked.

"Only when somebody gets killed; the police know where to find the dinghy motors. If the cruisers don't yell too much, they'll be sent over to me."

Señor Robados was unrestrained. He related a candid tale of small business chicanery. When the shower had passed, I was ready for some fresh air. Attempting to change the subject I told him that I needed some 2 cycle oil mix. He held up a liter bottle of oil.

"You mean like this?" he said. "That will be $15 dollars US."

"I'll go get my wallet" I said laughing. "I'll be back in a couple of weeks."

"Come back when you have a motor to trade" he replied with a mischievous grin.

Robados was a small greasy cog in an immense opportunistic machine which profits from suffering. The US Border Patrol reports that over 10,000 men, women and children are intercepted in their attempt to enter the United States via the Mona Passage. This number includes Cubans, Haitians and Dominican Republic nationals. The US Border Patrol does not publish records of rescues or estimates of drownings. Inequality and relative disadvantage are powerful motivators for emigration.

The first rays of the morning sun arched across the sky while Quest's Yanmar engine warmed to operating temperature. During our night sail to Playa Macao the previous evening, we had a minor mishap that would cause some inconvenience on our Mona crossing. Shortly after dark, a frigate bird had collided with the instrument cluster on the mast head. The frigate managed to sheer the wind transducer, VHF radio transceiver and navigational lights from the top of the mast. I did not take note of how the bird fared in the collision. In one quick stroke of a wing, we lost our ability to indicate our presence to oncoming boat traffic and to send and receive vital radio communication. The greatest inconvenience was the destruction of the wind transducer which displays the wind speed, wind direction and apparent wind direction. We

6

would have to do without the luxury of a small portion of our modern electronics. When we arrived in Puerto Rico the next morning, we would find out that the Border Patrol took a dim view of Quest crossing the Mona 'under the radar'.

With the anchor secured and pinned in the bow rollers I eased Quest through the reef at Playa Macao. Turning east, I raised the sails and engaged the autopilot. We were on our way. Would the god of the ocean blue be kind to us?

We were re-entering the United States a few years after a series of disastrous terrorist attacks sent shock waves through our society on September 11, 2001. As a result of this tragedy, US Immigration and US Customs had combined and morphed into a paramilitary force with a serious mandate and the muscle to back it up. Wendy and I had up-to-date passports. We had little to fear from Homeland Security, or so we thought.

In less than an hour we arrived at our first waypoint six miles east of the Dominican Republic. The sea was smooth and the wind light. Within an hour we would be crossing into the territorial waters of the United States. For the next six hours we sailed on a comfortable ocean with a full press of sail.

"So what's the big deal about the Mona Passage?" Wendy remarked.

"Be careful. It's a little early to be optimistic" I said.

Occasionally we were nudged off course by a strong transient current. In no time we were half way across the Mona without a single mishap.

"Well Captain, it's an hour before sundown. You were able to cook a great meal and bake a decent loaf of bread for supper, the wind is constant, and it's been a sweet trip on the good ship lollipop. We're only forty miles from Peppermint Bay. Are we allowed to be optimistic yet?" Wendy laughed.

"I have to admit that Mona didn't throw her worst at us. Let me see the chart" I said.

Our current course was laid down days ago. We were currently making a detour around a patch of permanently turbulent water near the Puerto Rican trench drop-off. The chart warned small craft to avoid an area of very rough water where the cold waters of the Puerto Rican trench meet the very warm waters of the Caribbean. The day's beautiful sailing conditions broke my resolve to play it safe with Mona.

"The water has barely a ripple" I said as I looked into the ocean. "I don't see any turbulent water. If we cut across here, we can cut more than an hour off the trip" I said pointing to the cautionary area marked on the chart.

"Let's do it" Wendy agreed.

After clearing the old waypoints on the GPS, I entered a single waypoint that would bring us within ten miles of the Puerto Rico coast. I changed course 20° to bisect the rough patch and re-trimmed the sails. Five miles into our new course, the sun was touching the western horizon. I congratulated myself on making a great decision to take the shortcut.

"I'm going to get some sleep" I said confidently. "Wake me in an hour."

I climbed down the companionway and lay on the settee. 'On the good ship lollipop, that's pretty funny' I thought to myself as I drifted off.

A half hour later I was jarred awake by what felt like a collision. I jumped up. I heard another great bang on the bow and was thrown back down onto the settee.

"What did we hit?" I yelled to Wendy in the cockpit.

I don't know. Come up here, something's wrong" she screamed.

I ran up the companionway. Quest was pitching and yawing violently and our speed had decreased. I took the portable spot light and shined the beam into the ocean. The ocean around Quest was a field of randomly spaced pyramidal shaped waves about seven to ten feet high. The pointed wave tops had no direction or pattern. I looked at the chart. We were right in the center of the rough patch. I turned off the autopilot.

"I'm going to try to steer around the worst of the waves" I said.

It was like trying to sail a toy boat in a washing machine. By three in the morning we had sailed out of the worst of the bumpy sea. When I relinquished the wheel to the auto pilot my shoulders and back ached. At sunrise the sea state was back to dead calm. I spread the chart on the cockpit table and looked at the course and time log for the night.

"Look at this Wendy. This is unbelievable. Would you have guessed that taking the shortcut through the washing machine would cost us an extra forty minutes?"

"Some shortcut" she agreed.

Quest for the Virgins

It was turning into a beautiful morning as we
paralleled the western coast of Puerto Rico. Except for the
three hour upper body workout at the helm, everything
went quite well. The green rain soaked hills of western
Puerto Rico seemed to be drawing us into their embrace.

"Look" Wendy said. "There's a sailboat gaining on
us."

"See if you can raise them on the radio" I said.

Wendy grabbed the VHF mike. Then she
remembered the missing antenna.

"You're a pretty funny guy" she said as she re-
clipped the mike.

"I'm going to slow down and let them catch up" I
said.

I brought Quest a few degrees into the wind and
the sails began to luff. The sailboat slowly grew nearer until
they came along our port side. The man in the cockpit
waved his radio mike in the air.

"Our radio is dead" I shouted back. "Come closer."

When our two boats had drawn close enough I
introduced myself.

"Did you cross the Mona last night?" I asked.

"Yes. How was your sail?" he asked.

"It was good" I answered.

"Something very strange happened last night" he
added.

"Did you go through a big patch of turbulence?" I
joked.

"No, I don't think so" he said with surprise.

"You would know if you did" I said.

Under the Radar

"No" he continued. "It was a lot stranger than a shoal. Around two in the morning, two US government launches came alongside and lit our decks up like Times Square. Then a group of armed men boarded and questioned us for a half an hour" he said.

"What did they want?" I asked.

"I have no idea. They never said. I can tell you, they were plenty scary."

"How so?"

"They acted like a SWAT team. Hey, we called ahead last night and arranged for a cab to bring us to Customs in Mayaguana this morning. Would you like to share the cab?"

"Sure" I said.

"Great, he's meeting us at the dinghy dock around nine o'clock."

"We'll see you there" I replied.

Two

Homeland insecurity

We soon found a good spot to anchor in the calm and very large Bahia de Boquerón. I threw a little water on my face and dressed for success. After listening to the frightening experiences with Homeland Security last night, I was not expecting a friendly handshake from Uncle Sam. Jean Pierre and Laura leaned against the taxi as Wendy and I approached in the dinghy. They greeted us warmly. Within minutes the four of us were on our way to the port city of Mayagüez which lay fifteen miles north of Boquerón. We expected our trip to US Customs and Immigration to be brief. Our courteous driver used all means at his disposal to shorten our cab ride. It was a journey to remember. Disregarding speed limits and all normal rules of the road, we zigzagged down the winding and narrow back roads of rural southeastern Puerto Rico in a teeth-clenching blur.

The Customs building in Mayagüez was a tastefully designed concrete bunker with a two foot sign above the doorway which read 'US Customs and Immigration'.

Homeland insecurity

"This is Customs and Immigration" the driver announced proudly in a thick Spanish slur.

His four passengers smiled and nodded. We were all glad that we had arrived without a fatality. He was an average maniac driver. He did possess better than average collision avoidance skills. If the Mona doesn't rattle you, try your luck with a Puerto Rican cab driver.

"Would you like me to wait?" he asked.

Our small entourage was composed of three Canadians and one American. Naturally everybody was waiting for someone else to make a decision.

Pierre spoke up first. "Please wait for us. We shouldn't be long. Where will you be parked when we are ready?"

The cab driver looked at us and waved his hands in the air. "I didn't mean that I was going to wait. I'm not going to wait here" he said in a placating tone. "What I meant to say was that I will come and pick you up. Just give me a call on my cell phone."

He snatched the money from Pierre and pressed a business card into his hand. He sped out of the parking lot, squealed around the corner and disappeared in a cloud of dust. We never saw him again.

Between stretches of blind terror on the ride to Customs, Pierre and Laura briefed us on their night visitation from Homeland Security.

"It was straight out of a movie" Laura stated excitedly. "Pierre was asleep in the saloon when 'wham', we were boxed in by two thirty foot patrol boats. They turned on all of their flood lights and ordered me to heave to. I luffed the sails. One of the boats pulled right up to our gunwales. The next thing I knew, three armed men in jump suits and black ski masks jumped into the cockpit. I screamed and Pierre tore through the companionway. They pointed assault rifles at Pierre and me and told us to sit on our hands in the cockpit."

"Did you offer them a cup of coffee?" I joked.

Pierre gave me a disapproving glance. "I think they already had too much coffee. I should have thrown a couple pounds of raw hamburger up the companionway" Pierre said.

I opened the door to let Wendy, Laura and Pierre enter. Mayagüez is a very busy marine port that serves much of western Puerto Rico. The presence of four cruisers in the lobby did not attract much attention. Pierre and Laura spotted a cruising couple that they had met in the Bahamas. Pierre made the introductions.

"Did you cross the Mona last night?" Pierre inquired of their friends.

The couple both nodded their heads and said in unison "We were boarded by armed border patrol."

I tugged on Wendy's sleeve and edged away from the group as the two couples exchanged their tales of frightening visits from masked men.

When we were out of earshot of the cruisers, I whispered to Wendy "Look, the only thing that we know about these four people is that they were both boarded by the same people that we're about to talk to. Let's check in first and keep our distance for the time being. Come with me, I'm going to check in" I said.

Homeland insecurity

I walked up to the counter and said good morning to the officer.

"Passports and boat name" he demanded with authority.

I handed him both passports.

"The name of our boat is Quest" I said.

He surreptitiously slid a computer printout from below the desk and ran his finger down a list of names.

"I didn't call ahead for a reservation" I joked.

"What day did you enter US waters and what was your last port?"

"We came from the DR last night, across the Mona" I said.

He looked back down at his printout. "What is the name of your boat again?" he said with a frown on his face.

"Our boat is Quest."

"Spell it" he said.

"Q U E S T."

Again he looked at the printout. "Are you sure that you came in last night?" he asked.

"Officer, we arrived in Puerto Rico from the DR about three hours ago."

"Step back from the counter and don't move" he said.

I complied. He reached up to his shoulder mic and with four words started a chain of events that would take two hours to unravel.

"Sir, we've got one".

A door opened behind the officer and a man with

lieutenant's bars stepped through. The junior officer turned around and spoke to the lieutenant.

The lieutenant addressed me.

"Are you the Captain of Quest?" he said.

"I am when she says I am" I said motioning to Wendy.

Customs agents are not a fun-loving bunch.

"Are you the Captain of Quest?" he asked again.

"Yes, officer" I replied.

"Is she a crew member?" he said pointing to Wendy.

"My wife" I said.

"Her name?"

"Wendy" I answered.

He turned and addressed Wendy. "Please remain seated on the bench against the wall Ms Wendy." He pointed at me and said "This way."

The interrogation room behind door number one was slightly more austere than the concrete gulag interior of the lobby. The room sported a nicotine-marinated, acoustic tiled ceiling which intersected with drab gray walls. An industrial grade faux-wainscoting extended the last three feet of the wall to meet a gray speckled tile floor much improved by years of wear and cigarette burns.

"Have a seat" he said pointing to a government-issued, pea soup green, plastic and chrome chair behind a table with a gray speckled Formica surface.

"Who's your decorator, the Marquis de Sade?" I asked trying to break down his icy demeanor.

He was not amused.

"So" he paused. "You say that you crossed the Mona last night?"

"I did" I said in a curt, friendly and most sincere manner.

Then he dropped the bombshell.

"There is no way that you crossed last night" he said while removing a sheet of folded paper from his coat pocket. He unfolded the paper, laid it on the table and slowly smoothed it with the side of his hand. "Now, let's take a look."

The Lieutenant was obviously enjoying this part of his job. He acted like a cat with a mouse trapped in the corner. Lieutenant Alvarez was playing his role perfectly. He managed to be scary and belligerent with a touch of sarcasm. His pace and timing was exquisite.

Attempting a flanking maneuver, I said "Have you been with Homeland Security very long?"

Handily deflecting my weak foray, he continued. "Quest isn't on this list."

He frowned and grinned at the same time. The room went silent. His short, definitive statement seemed to float above the table like a speech balloon. He stared at me. Our eyes locked. This was a moment for brevity. I placed both palms flat on the table.

"List? What list?" I said, maintaining a glassy stare.

"It's time we get to the point, Mister Beaupré. I have wasted enough time on this. Last night is old history, it's over."

"What's over?" I asked.

I could feel the blood rushing in my temples.

"There was a joint exercise conducted in the Mona last night" he said. He corrected himself. "We conducted an intercept exercise in the Mona last night. I was on one of the patrol boats."

"Hey, it was a great night to be out in the Mona" I said.

Lieutenant Alvarez ignored the remark. "Nothing got past our sweep, nothing" he said. "I have the list of all large and small craft that crossed the Mona last night."

"Can I take a look at your list?"

"No" he said, slamming his hand over the names.

"I am now going to tell you why I know you are lying. I just have to figure out why" he said. "All yachts have a VHF radio. Does your boat Quest have a VHF radio? How about a masthead light or a radar reflector? Any one of those would have given away your position if you really were in the strait last night" he said with a satisfied smirk.

So that's it, I thought to myself. "Quest doesn't have a radio, masthead lights or radar reflector" I said.

Lieutenant Alvarez stood up abruptly. I flinched.

"So you admit that you and your wife are smugglers. You admit to intentionally running under the radar."

He pressed a buzzer under the table. The ensign entered the room.

"We've got him."

"Hold on" I said. "Everybody take a breath here. Two nights ago while we were sailing to Playa Macao, a frigate bird sheared off the VHF radio antenna and mast lights."

18

The Ensign smiled and said "Sure, a bird ate his antenna. We can check that out easy enough sir."

Lieutenant Alvarez spun around. "How do you explain not having a radar reflector?" he said.

"That's really easy to explain" I said. "When I was equipping Quest I studied the radar signature of a mast with and without a deflector and there wasn't much of a difference. Deflectors also abrade the sail."

The Lieutenant had limited knowledge of sailboats. "What is he talking about?" he said to the Ensign.

"I think that he is saying that the reflector can rub a hole in the sail" the Ensign explained.

"Ensign Roberts will now escort you in the room behind that door" he said.

I got up and he opened door number two on the opposite side of the room. The room was about ten feet by ten with muted lighting. The interior decorators had outdone themselves with the paint palette. Radically contrasting gray and orange walls stood out against an austere table and chair.

"Sit down" the officer said.

He walked over to the wall and pulled a curtain back to reveal a one way mirror. He turned on a microphone.

"You're going to have a great view of the interrogation room from here. I designed this setup myself" he said with a roguish air of self satisfaction.

He left me alone in the room. There was no door number three to make an escape. I stared through the one way mirrored glass.

"Bring in the wife" were the next words that I heard over the wall speakers.

The Ensign went into the lobby. A moment later, Wendy entered the interrogation room. I ran the events of the last hour through my mind. I am in custody in Puerto Rico behind two sets of bolted doors and my future liberty depends on whatever Wendy says in the next thirty seconds. Wendy took her place at the table.

"Would you like a glass of water?" the Lieutenant asked.

"Do you have any herbal tea?"

He scratched the side of his head.

"Now, Wendy, that is your name?" He looked at Wendy's passport. "Where were you this morning around two AM?" Lieutenant Alvarez asked in a straightforward tone.

"I don't know" she said.

NO, NO, NO the voice screamed in my head. Lieutenant Alvarez looked at the Ensign and back to Wendy.

"Wendy, you don't know where you were last night?"

"I didn't say that" Wendy snapped.

'Slow down Wendy, you're doing great. Keep your cool' I whispered to myself.

"Well then, where were you at two AM?" he repeated.

"I don't know exactly. We were somewhere in the Mona. It was pretty rough. David had just made a snack and we were talking in the cockpit and…"

The Lieutenant cut her off politely. "That will be enough on that subject" he said. "Do you usually use your radio on night passages to talk to other boats?" he said with a smile.

"Always" she said.

'Tell him Wendy; tell him' I whispered fogging up the one way glass.

"So why was your radio turned off last night? The Mona is a pretty dangerous place, wouldn't you agree?"

"It's not too bad" she said. "There are some rough spots but overall it was easy. It was really pretty when the moon came out and…"

"About your radio, ma'am?"

"Oh that. That's what you want to know about. David said a frigate bird hit the mast two nights ago."

"David said? You weren't there?" he asked.

"I was there" she replied. "David said it was a frigate bird. He's never seen a frigate bird, especially one in the middle of the night. Maybe it was a frigate bird. It just kinda zoomed past us in the dark. What does he know about birds? I can tell you that something pretty big sure hit the mast. The whole boat shook when we lost the gear. It could have been a flying pig for all I know" she laughed.

"Why don't you have a radar reflector?" he asked.

"A radar reflector? You mean one of those over-priced tinfoil balls that you see in rigging?" she asked.

The Lieutenant stopped pacing the room and sat down. He put his hands over his eyes and mumbled to the Ensign "Let him out of there."

Was the matter settled to his satisfaction or were we about to be locked up in holding pens?

"Ensign, let Mr. Beaupré out" he repeated.

I was ushered back into the interrogation room.

"Please sit beside your wife" the Lieutenant instructed. "Did anybody see you in the Mona last night?"

We were finally getting somewhere, the all important eyewitness.

"There are two cruisers in the lobby that saw us in the Mona" I said.

"In the lobby?" he repeated. He stood up and walked to the wall. "Come here" he said.

He pulled a cord to open a double curtain which revealed yet another one way mirror.

"Hey, a see-through mirror, pretty cool. Can you get this at Home Depot?" Wendy said.

The Lieutenant looked at me and said "Point out the people that saw you last night."

"That's Pierre and Laura sitting over there against the wall. We met them this morning."

"Ensign, go meet and greet. Make absolutely sure that their boat is on the list."

"Yes sir."

"Ensign" I said. "I wouldn't bet that they can remember our boat name. None of us have slept in 24 hours. Ask them about the Bayfield 36 with the green stripe."

The Ensign looked at the Lieutenant. The lieutenant nodded OK.

We watched through the mirror as the Ensign

nonchalantly walked across the lobby with a distracted look on his face and engaged Pierre and Laura in conversation. Initially Pierre looked surprised then he smiled and nodded yes a few times. 'Thank you Pierre' I thought. The Ensign walked up to the mirror and pretended to be removing lint from his shirt. Then he looked straight through the mirror and gave the secret head nod. Lieutenant Alvarez walked to the table.

"Quest, right?"

"Yes" I said.

He leaned over the table and pulled the boat list towards him.

"Quest" he said as he wrote our boat name at the bottom of the list. "OK, we're done here. Don't forget to have your passports stamped before you leave the building."

"You look like you've been up all night. You should go home and get some sleep" I said.

"You look worse" he said and smiled. "You get some sleep."

"By the way Lieutenant, how many pirogues from the DR did you intercept last night?"

He looked at me. "We weren't really looking for pirogues. We were going for bigger fish. Have a nice visit to Puerto Rico" he said.

We walked into the gray light of the lobby. Pierre and Laura rushed up to us.

"What's going on? We didn't know whether to make a run for it" he laughed.

"Thanks for vouching for us" I said shaking his hand. "Let's get the cab driver down here."

"Well" Pierre said. "There's a little problem with the cabby."

"Problem? Did he have an accident?"

"I don't know if he had an accident, but it's very likely. I called him and he said that he wouldn't be coming, but he's going to send his brother. He said that his brother is a good driver ever since he had the accident and the cast came off."

Three

On a Mission of Masa

Our weary band of ocean cruisers stepped into the bright light. We edged our way from the intimidating concrete edifice of the Mayagüez Customs building. Pierre spotted a man asleep in a taxi under the shade of a banyan tree.

"I bet that's our man" Pierre said.

He walked up to the cab and tapped the trunk with his knuckle. The startled driver woke up and turned his head.

He winced in pain as he said "Hey, you Pierre? I'm Angel. My brother sent me to pick you up." He opened the Chevy's door and slowly lifted his left leg with two hands and gingerly placed his foot on the pavement. "My leg is killing me" he said.

"What happened to you?" Pierre asked.

"This is nothing" he said with pronounced bravado. "A gardening accident" he winked. "It doesn't hurt too much. The pain killers work pretty good if I drink some rum."

He held onto the car as he hobbled to the other side and opened the front passenger door. Holding his hand out for Wendy and Laura, he said "You two ladies can sit up here with me. You two sit in the back" he laughed.

His mood seemed to brighten when he sat in the driver's seat and started putting the moves on Laura. "You want I show you around tonight?" he said placing his arm on the back of the bench seat behind Laura's neck.

Laura turned her head towards Angel and slid her sunglasses to the bottom of her nose. "No" she said in an icy tone.

Angel turned to face the windshield and slowly pulled his arm back. Deflecting Laura's deep freeze, he looked in the back seat. "Hey, I could show you around Puerto Rico" he said. "It is very beautiful here this time of year."

Pierre wasn't falling for Angel's Latin charm. "When isn't it beautiful in Puerto Rico?" Pierre asked in a soothing voice.

"It is always beautiful in Puerto Rico. Sí. It is, well... more beautiful now" he said laughing and patting Laura on the knee.

"Is there a grocery store on the way to Boquerón?" I asked.

"Sí, sí, biggest supermarket in the Caribbean, the famous Pueblo Supermercado" he said putting emphasis on the 'supermercado'. "I go there all the time. It's a great store."

"Bring us to the store" I said.

"Wait a minute. Let me think. It's around here somewhere" he said with a questioning expression on his face.

We spent the next twenty minutes driving up and down back streets until he finally pulled up in front of a small kiosk in a residential area.

"I'll be right back" he said turning off the radio and pulling the keys out of the ignition.

Walking to the counter of the kiosk, he shook hands with the proprietor and offered him a cigarette and a pull from his rum bottle. The two men joked for a few minutes until Pierre poked his head out the rear window.

"Angel, we're waiting here" he said.

Angel waved his hand, smiled at Pierre and went back to his conversation. The car baked in the morning tropical heat.

"I'm getting out. I'll be sitting under the tree over there" I said.

Everybody opened their doors and stepped out. We started to cross the street when Angel abruptly cut off his conversation with the kiosk owner.

"Wait a minute" he shouted. "Don't you want to go to the Supermercado?"

He opened the front passenger door and smiled at Laura.

Laura looked at Wendy. "You first this time" she said.

Wendy got in and slid over. Laura got in the back seat. Just before Angel tried to shut the door, he ran his finger across her bare arm. Laura pulled her arm away and slammed the door.

"You're in luck. The Supermercado is only two streets over" he said to Pierre. "I don't know how I could have missed it."

"You go there all the time?" Pierre asked.

"Not to this Pueblo. I was thinking about the Pueblo in San Juan" Angel replied.

"San Juan is two hours from here, Angel."

"Yeah, it's a long drive. You want to go to San Juan? I guarantee that you will have a good time there. It's a real party town. I'll only charge you two hundred. That's a good deal. I'll throw in a half bottle of rum. My leg's getting tired. Maybe you can drive. This clutch is hard on my bad leg" Angel said to Pierre.

"The Supermercado" Pierre said.

We drove another two blocks. Angel pulled into the enormous parking lot of Pueblo Supermercado.

"See, I told you I knew where it was" Angel said proudly. "Do you want me to wait?"

Four voices rang out in unison "No!"

He grabbed the money that I held out and backed away from us, looking completely rejected. He took a swig of rum. His mood again brightened.

"Hey, it was really nice meeting you. If you need anything... you know... if you want to party" he said looking at Laura. "Give me a call."

He slowly left the parking lot and drove up the street in first gear. When we couldn't hear him anymore, Pierre let out a belly laugh. Then Wendy and I looked at each other and broke up. Laura did not laugh.

In front of the store, an old, well-weathered Puerto Rican grandmother sat under a threadbare Cinzano umbrella selling hot tamales from a pushcart.

"I'm going to get a tamale. Come over, I'll buy you one" Pierre said to the three of us.

We all walked over to the cart.

"Four tamales" Pierre said.

"Dos tamales" I said to the lady.

"You aren't hungry?" Pierre asked.

"Thanks for the offer. I'll pass, Pierre."

The toothless old lady grinned and slowly reached into the hot compartment of the cart. With trembling hands, she pulled out two tamales and handed them to Pierre and Laura.

"Wendy, ask her what are in the tamales" I said.

It wasn't the first time that I had seen a tamale. When we lived in Arizona, tamales were a staple. I had a fair guess what the ingredients were.

"Cómo se hace esto? (Do you make these?)" Wendy asked politely.

"Sí" Grandma replied with a smile. "Yo y mi hija (me and my daughter)."

"Ingredientes?" Wendy inquired.

"Mejores ingredientes (best ingredients)" she replied.

"Que?" Wendy asked.

"Carne de cerdo (pork meat) y manteca de res (beef lard)."

"No bacon fat?" I asked.

Wendy turned to the señora. "Sin grasa de tocino?"

"Sí, sí" she said. "Siempre utiliza la manteca de cerdo."

"You don't have to translate" I said to Wendy.

Pierre and Laura finished off the last of their tamales. Pierre looked at me and laughed.

"This is good pork." He licked his fingers. "Bacon fat really brings out the flavor of the lard. I think I'll get another" he said.

The smell of their tamale breath was a bit over the top.

"You know Pierre, you can make vegetarian tamales" I said.

"No" he corrected. "You can make vegetarian tamales. I'll stick to pork and lard" he said.

"Let me make a batch of veggie tamales for you tonight" I offered.

Laura agreed immediately.

"It looks like I'm outvoted" he said. "What kind of wine do you drink with veggie tamales, bacon-flavored chardonnay?" he joked.

"A good kosher tempranillo would suffice" I said. "Let's go inside and get some fresh air."

I opened one of the main doors to the supermarket.

The Pueblo Supermercado was not just large; it was intimidating. The fresh fruit and vegetable section was larger than some anchorages that we had been in. This was the biggest, best stocked grocery store that Wendy and I had seen in years. It exceeded the size of the average supermarket in south Florida. Laura and Pierre took the nearest cart and were lost in the maze of aisles in seconds. Our first mission was to provision Quest. The fun part would be to find the ingredients for the tamales. The only similarity between veggie tamales and pork tamales is the use of corn husks or plantain leaves and a lime-cured corn flour called masa harina. Making a tamale is simple. It does take time and practice to develop the skill to shape the masa harina dough and wrap it with the corn husks.

The recipe that I have managed to tune over the years begins with about a pound of masa harina. The flour is combined with cottage cheese, a pinch of baking powder, onion powder, parsley and salt. These ingredients are mixed together with a pastry blender. The cottage cheese gives the dough a smooth, firm, delicate consistency. A small ball of dough is flattened into an oval shape about six inches by four inches. A scoop of mashed cooked pinto beans, cooked carrots, raw onion and aged cheddar cheese are placed in the middle of the dough. The dough is folded over the vegetables and pinched shut into a tube shape. A corn husk is wrapped around the dough and tied shut with a narrow ribbon of corn husk. The tamale is then placed in a steamer basket and cooked until done. To eat the tamale, the corn husk is pulled back to reveal a fluffy moist dough exterior and a flavorful center of savory vegetables.

Pinto beans and masa flour are not hard to find anywhere in the world. I searched the entire store for the corn husks without luck.

"Where are the corn husks for tamales?" I asked the store manager. "This is Puerto Rico, right?"

He looked away in embarrassment. "There was a festival last week. We sold every corn husk and plantain leaf, even the ribbons. I'll have some Wednesday" he said.

"Thanks anyway" I said. Disappointed, I turned to put the tamale fixings back.

"Wait" he said. "You can always make a tamale pie. Use the same ingredients but layer them in a baking dish and put it in the oven."

I thought about it for a moment. "Excellent idea. Why didn't I think of that?" I said.

The excitement of having a new culinary door open gave me the necessary push to concoct an ad hoc recipe for veggie tamale pie. I already had the basic fixings from a well tested recipe. A bit of reverse engineering could transform a good, original recipe into a recipe of true merit: this was a matter of gastronomic pride. After all, it is an epic challenge to impress a Frenchman without using bacon fat. My 'mission for masa' entered the planning stage in the vegetable department.

A tamale is a very simple 'hand food'. After a cook has made a few hundred they can do it in their sleep. The tamale is about as complicated to eat as a hot dog with mustard. The one intriguing aspect of making a tamale pie was the infinite possibilities of vegetables that I could combine with the layers of masa dough. I selected fresh carrots and a bag of spinach for contrasting color and sweetness. Mushrooms fried and deglazed with red wine would contribute earthiness. Cooked masa dough can sometimes be dry. I picked a few very ripe tomatoes and a mild sweet onion for adding moisture between the layers. While I engaged in the 'tamale project', Wendy sorted through the seasonal varieties of tropical fruit.

"What about the beans, Wendy?" I shouted across the cathedral-sized fresh produce section.

"What about your beans?" Wendy said. "Can you say it any louder?"

Two young women suddenly looked up from a bin of plantains. I walked over to Wendy.

"A spicy black bean chili with TVP may be better than plain pinto beans" I said.

"You aren't going to find TVP in Mayagüez" she said.

"You're probably right" I agreed.

One of the young women pushed her cart over to

us and whispered "The TVP is in the cooler at the far back right corner of the store."

"Thank you" I said.

Fresh TVP in Puerto Rico, a vegetarian meat inspector in Luperón, 'what's the world coming to?' I laughed to myself.

On the way to the fresh vegetarian section, I collected a cart full of staples to resupply Quest's lockers. I ran into Pierre in the middle of aisle seven.

"Hey Pierre, how's the hunting?" I asked.

"I have something for you" he said. He produced a five pound can from his cart and handed it to me. "This is vegetarian lard" he said pointing to the label. "It's made from pigs that eat lettuce." He cracked up and pushed his cart away.

Vegetarians and herbivores need patience with meat-eaters. I found Wendy glassy eyed in the cookie aisle.

"Do you think we're done?" I asked.

"Sure" she said.

We rolled the cart to the checkout and had the bill tallied. While we waited for Pierre and Laura, I asked the store manager to call us a taxi.

The manger looked at me for a moment. "You've got to be kidding" he said. "Stick your head out the door and yell TAXI" he laughed.

I turned around to see Laura and Pierre paying for their groceries.

Pierre held up a smoked joint of pork. "Look, vegetable pig" he laughed.

"Ignore him" Laura said.

We pushed our carts out through the door.

"I thought that you were going to call a cab" Pierre said.

"Watch this" I said. I walked to the curb and yelled "TAXI!"

We heard four big V8 engines start. Within fifteen seconds we were surrounded by four cab drivers screaming at each other. Avoiding an incident, I pointed to one of the drivers. Hoping that I had chosen wisely, I said "Please bring us to the dinghy dock in Boquerón."

He walked around the Chevy opening all the doors. "I am Manny" he said.

"Drive slow. We would like to see the countryside" Pierre said from the back seat.

"I drive slowly" he said.

"Do you know Angel and his brother?" I asked.

The driver flicked his cigarette butt out the window. "Where did you meet those two clowns?" he asked.

I shrugged.

"They both drove cabs in Newark for a time. Nobody knows exactly what happened, but they came back to the island three months ago with pockets full of money. Angel was limping. Did he give you the hunting accident story?" he said with a laugh.

"Gardening" I said.

"America changes people" he said with resignation.

The drive back to Boquerón was a pleasant, calm experience with Manny at the wheel. He dropped us at the dinghy dock and kindly helped us with our groceries.

When we were settled in the dinghies, Pierre spoke

over the hum of the outboards. "We'll see you tonight about six."

"Six would be great" I said.

"I'll bring the bacon" he said.

Laura slapped him on the arm.

Back at Quest I immediately started the spicy black bean chili and the masa dough. Then I lay down in the berth for a nap. Wendy stayed awake to stir the chili. When the alarm sounded an hour later, the chili was cooked and the dough was soft and pliable. The masa dough was rolled into a 1/8 inch thick sheet. I cut and shaped the first layer into the bottom of the oiled pot. Layers of thinly sliced tomatoes were placed on the masa, followed by successive thin layers of spicy chili, carrots, canned sweet corn, wine-glazed mushrooms, steamed spinach, raw onion, fresh cilantro, cheddar cheese and another layer of masa dough. The layering was repeated until the pot was about three quarters full. It was topped with a thick layer of masa dough. The pie was lidded and placed on the lowest heat to cook for a couple of hours.

The lovely Laura and her jokester husband arrived as the sun was gently setting over the Bahia de Boquerón. The lush green hills of Puerto Rico were bathed in a soft champagne glow. We sat in the cockpit, enjoying each other's company after a very hectic day.

"Pierre, you've had a couple of drinks" I said. "Are you brave enough to try some tamale pie?"

We all went below.

"You do the honors" I said to Pierre. "Open the lid."

"This smells great. Can I have a small taste?" Pierre said.

"Of course" I said handing him a fork."

"Très bon, très bon" Pierre said. "It doesn't get any better than this. What a combination of flavors."

We took our places around the saloon table.

"To good friends and good food" Pierre said holding up a glass of good Tempranillo. "I have wanted to ask you this all morning" Pierre continued. "Wendy is from Boston and you're from Canada. How did you two meet?"

Four

Proposal on the Pyramids

"**W**ell Pierre, the short story is that we met in the Old Walled City of Jerusalem. A month later I proposed to Wendy on the Great Pyramid of Cheops in Egypt" I said.

"That's not a story. It's two sentences" Pierre said, pointing his finger at me.

"Jerusalem, the Pyramids, what a teaser. Tell us more" Laura said with wide eyes.

We left the dishes on the saloon table and adjourned to the cockpit. The twinkling lights of Boquerón shimmered off the calm waters of the bay under a cloudless night. Laura sat down on the cockpit cushions and drew her feet under her legs. Pierre sprawled the length of the bench with his head in Laura's lap. When he was finally comfortable, he raised his wineglass and said "Begin."

"It was back in the summer of '83" I said.

"Skip all the boring details" Pierre interrupted.

"No!" came the protest from the ladies. "We want to hear all the details" Laura said.

Proposal on the Pyramids

"In that case I'm going to pour another glass of wine" Pierre said getting up with a grunt.

"Can I finish the story Pierre?" I asked. He motioned with his hand to continue.

"In 1983, I had been traveling in the Mediterranean and the Middle East for about six months on a 'mission of discovery'."

"A mission of discovery" Pierre laughed. "I hate to burst your bubble but Neanderthals owned real estate in the Mediterranean 300,000 years ago."

"Thanks Pierre. If I may be permitted to continue… it was a mission of personal discovery. It was all new to me" I said.

"I was alone and traveling on the cheap. Before I met Wendy, I had been wandering for about six months. The last three months were spent hitch-hiking around Turkey and staying in remote villages. That was about all the dirt and diesel fumes that I could take. I was eager to expand my cultural and spiritual horizon in Israel. Before I tried to cross the border into Syria, I paid a brief visit to the First Secretary of the Canadian Embassy in Ankara. I wanted his advice about going from Syria to Jordan to Israel. He convinced me that crossing the border between Jordan and Israel was out of the question. The Canadian government had rescued six American hostages in Tehran in 1980. Canadian sentiment among our Arab brothers was running at an all time low. In the words of the First Secretary 'If you try to cross the Jordanian/Israeli border, don't expect me to show up to rescue you.'

39

On his advice, I island hopped through the eastern Mediterranean by private boat, ferry and airplane. I eventually arrived in the main Greek shipping port of Piraeus a month later. After a day of wandering the docks of Piraeus, I caught a ship bound for the Israeli port of Haifa. I bummed around Israel for a few weeks until I thought I was ready to see Jerusalem for the first time."

"You had to get ready to see Jerusalem?" Pierre questioned.

"Yes, I had to be ready."

"Do you mean because of the history?" Laura asked.

"No Laura, it wasn't the 300,000 years of history" I said winking at Pierre. "If you're ever lucky enough to visit Jerusalem, don't bring your opinions. You won't need them. There's too many there already" I laughed. "About two weeks before I met Wendy, I had taken a local bus from the Palestinian/Israeli village of Bethlehem" I continued.

"THE Bethlehem?" Laura asked.

"Yes. My host in Bethlehem dropped me off at the bus stop early in the morning. I took the first local bus that was headed to the Old City. I paid the fare and asked the Arab bus driver to drop me off anywhere close to the 'Old City'. Twenty minutes later he stopped the bus and opened the door. He pointed to me and announced 'David's Gate.' I stepped out of the bus and stared at the beautiful walled city of old Jerusalem."

"Wait a minute, David's Gate? You've got to be kidding" Pierre said.

"Yes, it was a bit bizarre. All the gates in the Old

City have a name. David's Gate is one of eight gates leading into the Old Walled City of Jerusalem. David's Gate is also known as the Jaffa Gate or The Golden Gate.

The first thing I always did in a new place was to find lodging so that I could drop my bag. As I walked through David's Gate, my mind reeled at the thought of the history that had taken place within these walls. I wandered up David Street in awe. It was utterly fantastic, 'the cradle of civilization'.

I hadn't gone six hundred feet before I spotted a run-down hotel with the ridiculous and most unlikely name of 'Swedish Youth Hostel'. I walked through a half open door and climbed a flight of stairs. The proprietor, Josef, sat in front of a small TV watching a soap opera."

"Hello, hello" he said giving me a weak handshake.

"Swedish Youth Hostel...are you Swedish?" I laughed.

"No, I'm Palestinian. Don't laugh. It's a great name, great for business. It got you to come in."

"No" I said. "It's in my price range."

"Cheap and Swedish, what a combination" he said, showing me to the men's dormitory on the second floor. It was a dark, dank hole with twenty threadbare beds arranged in barracks fashion.

"The women's room and wash room are on the third floor" he said with a wink. "Throw your bag under that last bed. Come and have a cup of mint tea."

I lifted the wrought iron leg of the bed and ran it through the handles of my bag. I snapped on a padlock and chain for good measure.

"You don't need to lock your stuff up. I watch everything" he said with pride.

Josef was a pleasant host. The Swedish Youth Hostel was a comfortable, cheap fleabag in a magnificent ancient city. I had limited trust in Josef and the impoverished expat clientele.

The Old Walled City of Jerusalem is a fortified city built by the Ottoman Empire in the mid 1500's. The walled city is a half mile by half mile square. When the pack was safely locked up, I was free to explore the meandering maze of streets and alleyways. I left the doorway of the Swedish Youth Hostel and turned left onto David Street.

Proposal on the Pyramids

Old Jerusalem is a 6000 year old city still brimming with vivacity. It is a city of good people and bad, trying to live their lives surrounded by war and hatred. They vie for existence in a confined space with overlapping and feuding ideologies. Merchants selling wares of all description cram tiny store fronts and sidewalks with pots, pans and fluorescent plastic statues of Jesus from China. Elaborate, tacky depictions of decapitated saints painted on black velvet are draped on cheap wooden frames beside a shop that sells women's high-heeled leather boots from Brazil.

The most outlandish tourist schlock is reserved for the most devout and artistically challenged of the faithful who are drawn to the 'Via Dolorosa'. The Way of the Cross begins in a parking lot in the Armenian Quarter and serpentines through the alleys of the Old City to the

Church of the Holy Sepulcher. The entire meandering route of the Via Dolorosa is scattered with eager entrepreneurs selling low quality souvenirs to the devout pilgrim. Shop after shop sells the same plastic crucifixes and bottles containing an actual fragment from the 'Cross of Jesus'. You absolutely can't go back to Montana without buying the original spike that impaled the right hand of Jesus. It is enterprise. It is religion. It is show business. So you want Judas's thirty pieces of silver in their original leather purse? At the current spot price of silver, it is yours for $438 US, unless you can strike a better deal down the street.

The city is only one square kilometer in area, a mere 220 acres. Despite its size, religious rivalry has managed to chop the city into four distinct cultural zones. Christians, Jews, Armenians, and Muslims all claim a quarter and exert quasi-sovereignty over their slice of the holy city. The city is a living shrine and a battleground for the religious intolerant. It is a pressure cooker for conflicting ideologies whose differences are often indistinguishable.

The Jews and the Arabs contribute the lion's share to the 6000 year old brawl. Within the walls of the Old City, a peace that prevailed on Monday can give way to war and bloodshed on Wednesday, then back to business as usual on everybody's Sabbath. The residents learn to live and love in a small world with uneasy certainties. The man that shook your hand this morning may be your mortal enemy by sundown. An unintended slight between merchants or an off-handed comment from an Israeli soldier can blow the lid off the pressure cooker. To an outsider like me, the conflict and overlapping discord seemed to be controlled anarchy within a framework of chaos.

I began walking up David Street towards the Arab Quarter when I got the strange feeling that I was being followed. I walked ten paces and looked at my reflection in a shop window. Two young Arab boys stood across the alleyway checking me out. I turned around quickly. They ducked into a doorway. At first glance they looked about eight years old. Walking another block, I slipped around a corner. A moment later the two street ruffians walked by.

"Hello" I said. "Something I can do for you boys?"

"Mister, we weren't following you, really we weren't."

"You weren't following me?" I said.

"No Mister, no way, we're just going to my father's shop."

"Good" I said. "Bring me to you father."

"You want to buy carpet?" one of the boys asked.

"I don't know, maybe" I said. "We'll see."

They both looked ready to bolt at any moment. Then the smaller of the boys looked up at me with an entrepreneurial eye.

"OK Mister, follow me."

After a couple of turns down blind alleys, the two boys motioned for me to enter a carpet shop. As I crossed the threshold of the shop, the owner looked at me and frowned.

"What did he do this time?" he said.

I smiled and held out my hand in greeting.

"You want to buy a Persian carpet? These are from Persia. I don't sell that Chinese junk."

"No" I said. "I don't need a carpet."

The store owner looked at me blankly. "You Mossad" he laughed.

"No, definitely not Mossad" I said. "I could use a couple of smart kids to show me around the Holy City."

The merchant turned around seeming to ignore me and started to arrange a pile of kilims. 'This isn't going very well' I thought to myself as I started to back out of the shop.

He turned suddenly and said "Great idea. This one is Ahmed and the other is my sister's boy Amir. Show the man around the Old City and don't get into any more trouble" he said, cuffing Ahmed on the back of the head. "And don't pester him for baksheesh" he warned. "When you've seen enough history, come back and buy a carpet" he said with a smile.

Each boy grabbed one of my hands, pulled me through the shop door and down the street towards the Christian Quarter. I reined them in when we came to the tourist entrance for the Church of the Holy Sepulcher.

"Come" Ahmed said. "We show you the easy way in." He tugged on my shirt and led me around another corner. "Stick the ball cap in your pocket and put this on" he said handing me a yarmulke. "Follow me."

"What's the yarmulke for?" I asked.

"Camouflage" he said. "Walk fast through the door and don't stop if someone talks to you."

Proposal on the Pyramids

The Artful Dodger looked around cautiously, then motioned Amir and me to follow him. I wasn't sure how two Arab boys and a westerner wearing yarmulkes was much of a disguise in a Christian church but it seemed to work. No one paid us the slightest bit of attention. As soon as we came into the main body of the church, Ahmed cleared his throat and started on a well rehearsed tour guide speech.

"Where did you learn all of this stuff?" I said.

"We follow the tour guides" he said.

The boys' animated tour was a wonderful combination of showmanship, ridiculous inaccuracies and completely fabricated Christian mythology. At eight years old, he already had all the makings of a superb carpet salesman. When we came to the orthodox section of the church, Ahmed grabbed my hand and pulled me aside.

"You got to see this. He does this every day" he said.

I watched as a group of American women walked up and stood in front of a small side altar. An ancient, grizzled orthodox priest in full regalia greeted them. We drew closer to the women.

"He's going to tell them to get on their knees and kiss the rock in front of the altar. Then he's going to bless them" Ahmed said laughing.

"What's so funny about that?" I said.

"Wait until you see how he blesses them" he said.

As each woman knelt down on both knees to kiss the stone, the priest put his left hand on their head and whispered a blessing in their ear.

47

"I still don't get it" I said.

Ahmed looked at me in the dim light and frowned. "Don't look at his left hand. Watch his right hand" he said.

Sure enough, each time a woman knelt and kissed the floor the priest put his left hand on her head. At the same time that he brought his mouth close to her ear to give the holy invocation, his right hand slid between the woman's legs.

"Wait, wait, here comes the best part" Ahmed said.

When the priest was finished molesting the seven women, they gathered around him. As if a quick bum grab wasn't enough, he held out his hand for donations. The group dutifully opened their purses and gave generously.

"That's what I want to do when I grow up" Ahmed said with a sigh.

"Forget it, Ahmed. You're eight years old" I said.

After giving Ahmed an hour to completely misrepresent 2000 years of church history, we followed a tour group out through the main ornate entrance of the Church of the Holy Sepulcher. Outside in the bright light, Ahmed and Amir demonstrated complete ease with the tourists. They spent another uninhibited half hour hamming it up in front of the tourists' cameras before we left for our next stop.

For the next few days, I met the boys in front of the carpet shop before it opened. They showed me around the well trodden streets and their secret places in the Old City. As soon as I knew the Old City like the back of my hand, it was time to move on and travel to the resort city of Eilat on the Red Sea. I was up early in the morning with my bags packed and ready to leave for the bus stop when the owner entered the common room.

"Ah, you are leaving. Have a cup of tea before you go?"

"Sure" I said.

I sat down in a sagging plastic lawn chair and started to talk to Josef when three girls fresh off the plane from JFK walked up the stairs. Josef jumped up and started to put on the charm.

"How long are you going to stay at my famous Swedish Youth Hostel?" he asked.

"We want to see the Via Dolorosa and the Dome of the Rock" one of the girls said.

Another chimed in "Don't forget the Western Wall and Church of the Holy Sepulcher. It shouldn't take more than a day."

I looked at Josef, then back to the girls. "You're going to see all of the Old City in one day, maybe have a falafel for lunch?" I said with a hint of skepticism.

One of the girls looked at me and said "Sure, that's enough time."

"That's only enough time to get lost" I said.

I shouldn't have opened my mouth.

Josef looked at me and said "David can show you around the city, couldn't you?"

"OK, come on" I said begrudgingly. "I'll give you the fifty cent tour."

I checked back into the hotel and spent the next two days playing tour guide. On the second day, I showed them the Via Dolorosa.

Quest for the Virgins

We were just coming up to the Fifth Station of the Cross, when I stopped the group and said "This is where Simon of Cyrene took the cross from Jesus and ran down that alley over there." I pointed to a souvenir store. "That's the famous Fifth Station Souvenir shop" I said with a straight face.

Two of the girls looked at me and politely nodded their heads. Wendy stifled a belly laugh. The two other girls went back to their conversation.

Wendy walked up to my side and said in a low voice "You've been making fun of us all this time. I don't blame you. We must seem ridiculous. I just met them yesterday."

Wendy and I soon ditched her new acquaintances and headed out alone. Wendy and I started a relationship that day that has managed to endure for more than thirty years. She had come to Israel for a month, planning to spend some time on a kibbutz.

"Hey" I said to Wendy one evening while we were sitting on the holy grass in front of David's Gate. "I'm going to Egypt soon. Do you want to come?"

"The Pyramids?" she asked.

"There's plenty to see in Egypt, Pyramids and more" I said.

"Sure I'd love to go" she agreed.

"After Egypt, I'm going to Germany to wait for the rainy season to end in Nepal. Then I'm flying to Kathmandu."

"Wow, that's so cool" Wendy said.

"Why don't you come to Nepal with me?"

Proposal on the Pyramids

Wendy let go of my arm and backed away. "I have to go back to law school in September" she said.

"No you don't."

"Yes I do" she argued.

"Look, law school can wait. You might not get another chance to see Nepal" I said with a grin.

She smiled, reached up and kissed me. "OK I'll go to Nepal with you."

Before the week was up we crossed the border into the Gaza Strip by foot. We hailed one of the many cab drivers that wait just inside the Egyptian border. He brought us to Cairo and dropped us in front of a cheap tourist hotel. The next day at dawn we caught the local bus that brought us close to the Pyramids. The Pyramids looked small from two miles away. Every step on the dusty road to the entrance brought the grandeur of the Pyramids into perspective.

After paying a small fee, we walked up to the base of the huge main Pyramid of Cheops.

"Let's climb to the top" I said.

"We can't climb to the top" Wendy said. "Look at the signs."

There were signs every fifty feet around the Pyramid warning visitors not to climb or deface the pyramids under penalty of law.

"Let's give it a shot anyway" I said.

"Not me" she responded.

I strained to climb the first giant block of stone. "Come on."

I held out my hand. She frowned and climbed up beside me. We climbed to the second block before the guards arrived.

"Get down, get down. We arrest you."

We climbed down and the Guard began to scream at us. "Are you crazy? Can't you read the signs? Come with me. I'm taking you to my supervisor."

"Wait a minute" I said to the guard. "I was climbing the Pyramid so that I could propose to her at the top" I said producing a pop top ring from a soda can.

He looked at me for a second. "You are kidding. I have been here for ten years. I never saw anybody get engaged here. Fantastic! Well, go ahead" he said.

I turned to Wendy and put the pop can ring on her finger. "So have I asked you to marry me yet?" I said.

"No, but close enough" Wendy said.

Laura got up. "That is about the most romantic story I have ever heard" she said hugging Wendy.

Pierre rolled over and let out a laugh. "Not bad" he said. "Come on Laura, it's time to go home.

They slipped over the stern of Quest into their dinghy.

"Maybe we'll see you down island" he said shaking my hand.

"I am sure that we will. I'm glad we met" I said.

They disappeared into the darkness.

Five

Fear of Falling

The Boquerón anchorage was silent as Pierre and Laura sailed past Quest the next morning. They waved from the cockpit as their sails luffed in the light breeze. Clearing the harbor and turning south, their boat became a tiny dot and slowly disappeared over the horizon. They were gone.

"The party's over. It's time to get some work done" I said.

Today's objective was to climb to the mast head and survey the damage that the frigate bird had wrought on our instruments when we were sailing in the DR.

Climbing the mast is an unavoidable task for a cruiser. The mast head of a modern cruising sailboat is a very populated piece of real estate. There is a full complement of navigational lights and instrumentation on the mast head of a well-equipped cruising boat. This equipment normally requires little maintenance. The very top of an aluminum mast is smaller than a ten inch oval. All four halyards have a dedicated sheave. All of the running rigging that hold up the mast is terminated at the mast head. Wind transducers, navigational lights and radio antennae are also bolted to the very top of the mast. With all this vital equipment in one place, something is bound to break and need to be replaced. Only an imprudent captain is not prepared to climb the mast in an emergency.

Climbing a very smooth, slippery, aluminum oval pipe with a cross section of nine inches and rising to a height of fifty feet is a task to be approached with forethought and caution. Getting to the top is relatively easy compared to conducting a repair with both hands free. A repair may have to take place in rain, gale force winds and pitching seas. A few people, though not many, take to this difficult task with ease. I and the majority of sailors do not.

Before buying Quest I never thought that I was afraid of heights. It was the aftermath of a very bad hail storm that brought my aversion to heights into focus. I did not have an irrational fear of heights. I like to think that I had a normal, rational fear of falling to my death. I was working in the interior of Quest in Charlotte when a bad storm blew in. Hail began to pelt the decks. At first the noise of small pellets hitting the deck was almost imperceptible. In only a few minutes the hail was the size of golf balls. The noise in the saloon was deafening. Quest came through the storm without a scratch. Our house was about three hundred feet from the boat. Quest may have been spared but our roof was ruined. The hail had destroyed the shingles to the point that the damaged roof needed immediate replacement.

A few days later the roofers were busy tearing off the old roof when they discovered a couple of rotted substrate boards.

"Maybe you should come up here and see this" the crew foreman shouted.

Why did this rotten board have to be at the highest and steepest part of the roof? I climbed the shaky ladder up 25 feet, carefully stepped on the roof and climbed to the peak.

"Replace it" I said.

Then I turned around and looked thirty five feet down to the driveway. I froze and sat down.

"You OK man?" the foreman asked.

The entire crew of ten men stopped and waited for the gringo to pitch head first into oblivion. Sensing my panic, the foreman and two of the roofers grabbed my arms, turned me around and helped me onto the ladder like a stiff cadaver. The first thing I thought when reaching the ground was 'how am I going to climb a mast that is fifty feet above the decks?' All current projects were shelved until I could solve this overarching concern.

The most simple and common method of reaching the top of the mast is to attach a bosun chair to a halyard and be pulled up. It is very dependable. It does require the help of another person to work the halyard. Installing folding mast steps all the way to the top is the most costly and labor intensive solution. It is also the safest, fastest and easiest way for a person to climb the mast unaided. The installation requires drilling and tapping about 200 holes in the mast, four for each step. The mast steps are screwed in place with permanent loctite to halt possible electrolysis between the aluminum mast and the stainless steel screws.

Climbing the mast with the use of mast steps is a one person job. The only additional equipment is the safety harness that attaches to the torso. A safety tether encircles the mast and is attached to the harness at the climber's waist. In order to work 'hands free' at the mast head, the tether is adjusted so that one can stand securely on the steps and lean back, placing all of the body weight against the tether. It takes practice, agility and an iron nerve to lean back and put your trust in a small nylon line while fifty feet above a pitching deck.

The weather in Boquerón's anchorage was perfect when I climbed the mast to assess the frigate's damage. The wind was mild and the anchorage calm. I wasn't surprised when I saw that the mast lights and wind transducer were gone without a trace. The radio antenna was broken and hanging by a single wire. I removed the broken gear and covered the mast head with a garbage bag to keep it dry.

With ready access to phones, the US Postal Service and couriers, Puerto Rico was a very good place for us to make the needed boat repairs. Besides repairing the electronics, we also had to find a sail loft. Wendy and I had removed all the headsails in Mayaguana in the Bahamas to make an emergency repair. Two months later, our hand stitched repairs had frayed badly. With the help of the Boquerón marina, we found a sail loft in Salinas, a small city halfway along the southern coast of Puerto Rico.

My first call was to the Salinas sail loft.

"What exactly is the problem with your sails?" the loft owner asked.

"The sun stripe stitching seems to be rotting away."

"Rotting? Who sewed the stripe?" she asked.

"It was a loft in Pennsylvania."

"Pennsylvania?" she repeated. "That's way north. I didn't know they had boats up there" she said joking.

"The Chesapeake has plenty of boats" I said.

"Oh yeah, the dinghy fleet" she said. "We have one thing in Puerto Rico that they wish they had in Pennsylvania."

"What's that?" I asked.

"Three hundred and sixty-five days of heat and sun. That's what ate up the stitching on your sun stripe. I bet they didn't use UV coated thread. You're going to need it here. Bring your sails in. I'll rip out all the stitching and replace it with a thread that will give you about ten years of life in the tropics. What's the color of your sail stripe?" she asked.

"Green" I said.

"Light green, dark green? It doesn't matter" she said. "I don't have any green. I can't remember ever using green" she said.

"You never use green?" I asked.

"No green" she said. I could hear her in the background searching in a box. "I've got fifty shades of blue."

"Forest green" I said hopefully.

"Forest green" she replied. "No, I don't have any forest green" she said winding up for the sales pitch. "I could replace your stripe with blue cloth. It would look pretty sharp. Almost everybody has a blue stripe. It looks great in the Caribbean."

"No" I said. "We'll stick with green."

"Well, that's going to be a problem. I'll have to order a large spool" she said.

"So order a spool."

"That's the problem. It has to be shipped from Europe, there's VAT, import tax and then there's the quantity. If I order green thread, I have to buy a whole spool."

"OK, I'll pay for the spool" I said.

"Sure, I'll order it today."

I hung up the pay phone and laughed to myself. It was actually faster and cheaper to replace the sail stripe cloth than order a spool of thread - welcome to the Caribbean.

The next call was to Raytheon Marine in the US. I thought that I had saved the easy call for last. What could be so hard about ordering a replacement part from one of the world's premium marine instrument makers? Phone the 800 number in the manual, give them a part number and your credit card and they ship it. My naïve optimism went unrewarded.

Fear of Falling

When we bought Quest, I gave up on the notion of trying to save the original instruments. The electronics were fourteen years old and looked like museum pieces. On our survey trials off the coast of Fort Lauderdale, the instruments had consistently malfunctioned. My plans to recondition the instruments came to a halt when I found out that they would be cheaper to replace than fix. The old instruments were unceremoniously boxed and placed in the trash. Re-equipping Quest with state-of-the-art modern electronics would be a fun voyage into the netherworld of overpriced consumer gadgetry.

The pleasure of buying a complete instrument package would not be complete without a trip to a big boat show. Wendy and I took a leisurely 600 mile drive to the St. Petersburg, FL boat show. Attempting to avoid the press of a large crowd, we arrived at the event early on a Monday morning. As soon as I walked through the doors of the boat show, I knew I was over my head. I was definitely not a sailor. At best I was a boat tinker. The St Pete boat show is for real sailors. Feeling a bit overwhelmed I kept my head down and searched for the Raytheon (Raymarine) booth. Except for a few early risers the show was dead. As would be expected from Raymarine, their booth was a cavernous light and sound show that would befit the bridge of a sci-fi movie set. We were immediately approached by a member of the Raymarine sales team. He was short, thin and wore his ghostly white pallor with ease. He was definitely not a ruddy faced yachtie fresh from an America's Cup race.

"How can I help you folks? I'm Jason. I work in Raymarine R&D."

Quest for the Virgins

"We have to replace our entire instrument package" I said.

"Great" he said with a happy grin. "What type of sailing do you do?"

I avoided any possible faux-pas by saying that we wanted to see the most state-of-the-art instruments that Raymarine sold for cruising boats. The state-of-the-art part was music to the techie ears.

"You two are making the right decision" he said nodding. Guiding us to the back of the tent, he pulled a white tarp off the ST80 display. "Check this out" he said as he flipped a switch. The display lighted up like the bridge of a thousand foot oil tanker. "These are the most advanced instruments that Raymarine sells in the consumer market. I helped design the screen" he said with pride. "This is the future of marine instruments. Everything was developed from the ground up."

We listened to his pitch for the next half hour. They were definitely state-of-the-art. Instead of using dedicated displays, all the data was displayed on a single multi-view screen. These common screens could display all data and be placed anywhere on the boat. All the boat's data could be accessed by paging through screens rather than having a dedicated wind, depth and speed display. It was very impressive.

"Do you sell many of these ST80's?" I asked.

"We sold some to racing teams. Other than them, I don't know. The system is beautiful. It's just a little complicated for the average boater" he said.

"We'll be back" I said.

Wendy and I discussed it for a couple of minutes. We both came to the conclusion that 'complicated' was good. We walked back to the salesman who was still playing with the ST80 instruments.

He took one look at our smiles and said "You won't regret buying the ST80's. It's a good thing you came today. This is the only day I'm at the show. The other salesmen are on commission. They never show the 80 series. They only want to sell the ST60's."

"Why?" I asked.

"You know salesmen. What do they know about instruments? They only sell what they understand."

Wendy pulled out the credit card and bought the most state-of-the-art system on the market.

The Raytheon ST80 was unceremoniously pulled off the market the following year due to abysmal sales figures. The geek was right. The average boater didn't warm up to a system that required an engineering degree to operate. On the other hand, the system was so robust that I never would have learned that the ST80's were mothballed if the frigate bird had not collided with the mast.

Being hit by a bird at night is unquestionably a rare event. Rare or otherwise, that is why I found myself still standing in a phone booth in the noonday tropical sun in Boquerón, Puerto Rico. I dialed the 800 number for Raymarine.

"This is Raymarine. How can I direct your call?"

"I need to speak to someone about a replacement part" I said.

I was connected to the sales department.

"I need a mast head wind transducer for an ST80 system" I said.

"Sorry… we stopped making the ST80 system two years ago."

"Two years ago? I only bought it three years ago."

"That's too bad" he said. "It was a great system. We sold a few to the U.S. America's Cup team. The average boater never really liked them, they were way too advanced" he said.

"I need a replacement part" I said.

"We don't keep obsolete parts in stock. It's funny" he mused. "The most advanced system we've ever sold and it's obsolete. Go figure."

It was ironic but it wasn't funny at the moment. "I still need a replacement wind transducer" I said pleading.

"I wish I could help you. Hey… I've got an idea. Hold on, I'm going to call Bill in Repair." I baked in the phone booth for another five minutes. "Bill's on the line. He might be able to help you. He's the supervisor in repair."

The salesman dropped off. "I'm Bill. What's going on?" he said in a withering tone.

"I'm in Puerto Rico and I need a new wind transducer for an ST80."

"ST80, man we haven't seen those in a while" he said. "How did you break one of those? They're carbon fiber. They're indestructible."

"A bird took it out" I said.

"That's a good one. A bird ate my wind transducer. You say you're in Puerto Rico?"

"Yes."

"I bet it's really nice. What race did you say you were in?"

'Race… he thinks that I am in a race' I thought. This could work. "We are in the Race for the Virgins" I said.

"Race for the Virgins…real catchy name. I've never heard of that one. What's your boat name?" he asked.

"Quest, she's 12 meters" I said.

"So, she's in the twelve meter class. How's the race going?"

"Real slow" I said, laughing to myself. Wendy and I made about one hundred miles to the good a month.

"Hold on" he said. "I think I remember using an ST80 wind transducer on top of the Christmas tree last year. Let me check. Call me back in ten."

"Quest?" he said when he answered the phone. "Yeah, it was in with the Christmas decorations. You still want it? I'll test it for you. I think we still have the test jig."

"Of course" I said.

"Give me your address and I'll ship it to you. I can't charge you for the transducer. It doesn't show up in inventory. Just pay for the shipping. Hey, a little Christmas present in March" he said. "The next time you're in the US, buy us a new angel for the top of our Christmas tree" he laughed.

Six

It's My Island Now

With all the repair parts ordered, we went on our way to pick them up in Salinas. We quietly slipped out of the peaceful sea resort of Boquerón and sailed south. Our first course would bring us to Cabo Rojo on the southwest corner of the island. Sailors rounding Cabo Rojo in the early morning light have a treat for the eyes. The red-tinted cliffs appear to catch fire in the orange glow of dawn. The high cliffs of Cabo Rojo jut far out into the Caribbean. We sailed as close as we dared to the looming cliffs. Up ahead and beyond the shelter of Cabo Rojo, the Caribbean Sea was being whipped into a turmoil of froth and breaking waves by the twenty mile per hour trade wind. I loosed the head sail just before the first gusts blasted our broadside. Quest barely heeled. A course change of ninety degrees east into the trades brought her close into the wind. We were in for a short, wet and windy sail to the small village of La Parguera which lay only ten miles up the stormy windswept southern coast of Puerto Rico. La Parguera is a reef strewn bay in which Columbus took refuge before greeting the friendly Taíno Indians.

Christopher Columbus is the westerner who discovered what we call the island of Puerto Rico. During his second journey to the Americas on November 19, 1493, the 30,000 Taíno natives were enjoying an advanced agrarian civilization on their island paradise. Columbus reported that the natives were unafraid of the landing party. How dangerous could twenty emaciated white men in bright red satin underwear and funny hats possibly be to mighty Taíno warriors?

What Columbus said to the thousands of friendly Taíno people crowding the south shore of Puerto Rico in 1493 is not known. There is room for speculation. He was no doubt greeted by the local tribal chiefs with kindness and open arms. What we know for certain is that he was not reading from a bad Hollywood script. If he were, all the smiling Indian faces would have turned his way in supplicating reverence. He would wait for the cheers of his admirers to quiet down. Then with perfect timing, he would cup his hands to his mouth. He would enunciate in precise Portuguese. His voice would carry over the heads of the crowd and reverberate off the dry hills of the south coast of Puerto Rico. The message would have been short and to the point.

"OK people, it's my island now. We're going to call it San Juan Bautista."

Columbus would go on to explain their mutual positions. The Spaniards and the sovereign king of Spain expected great things from the Taíno Indians.

"Work hard, give us all your gold and food, act like good Christians and when you die, we will reserve a special place in heaven for you."

The Taíno were no doubt impressed by Columbus' pomp, pageantry and straightforward delivery. The part about becoming the newly acquired slaves of Columbus and the King of Spain was probably glossed over by the translator.

Columbus didn't have much time for small talk when he landed on the south shore of Puerto Rico. He was in a bit of a rush, having two more islands to conquer before supper. After delivering his stirring oration to the Indians, he then turned to Ponce de Leon and the crew.

"We're outta here. Back in the boats, boys. Time is money."

The Taíno were in no hurry. They had plenty of time to ponder the outcome of their first encounter with Europeans. Columbus' log records an initial stay of only two days in Puerto Rico. Columbus and the Spaniards then ignored the island of San Juan Bautista (Puerto Rico) for over ten years until Ponce de Leon was granted governorship of the island in 1509.

Before Columbus dropped by, the island of Puerto Rico was known to the Taíno people as Boriquén. The Taíno prospered and built cities with advanced agricultural methods. Before the Taíno, the island was first inhabited by the Ortoiroid people between 3000 and 2000 BC. The Saladoid Indians populated the island between 430 BC and 1000 AD. The Taíno in Puerto Rico are the descendants of the Ortoiroid and Saladoid Indians.

It's My Island Now

The Spanish finally renewed their interest in Puerto Rico in 1508. King Ferdinand dispatched Captain Yañez Pinzón to establish a military presence. Ponce de Leon followed the next year to represent the Crown as the island's anointed governor with a personal interest in discovering the Fountain of Youth. On arriving in the New World, Ponce de Leon followed 'The Conquistador's Standard Manual for Success in the New World'. First, convince the Indians that you are immortal gods. After the initial break-in period, expect half the indigenous population to die from European diseases. The first two phases of the plan went perfectly. The Taíno had a bit of trouble converting to Christianity. They weren't bad fort builders and they knew how to grow the food that sustained the Spaniards. After a few years of being dutiful slaves to the Europeans, the Taíno began to question the divinity of their Spanish masters. Were the Spanish really gods, the Taíno asked themselves. Even though the Indians were pushovers for officers in gold braid and shiny hats, they did possess the power of reasoning to determine the divinity of the conquistadors. They devised a simple test to establish the divine providence of the conquistadors: hold one of the gods under water for a couple of hours. If he died, he was mortal.

On a splendid day in 1511, the Taíno Chief Urayoán ordered his people to put on a lavish celebration. He invited the legendary Spanish conquistador Diego Salcedo to attend. Don Diego Salcedo was not the type of gentleman to miss a great feast in his honor. When Urayoán's warriors showed up in the Spanish encampment to escort Don Diego to the festival, he was dressed in his frilly fineness. They carried him back to the village with the honor befitting a god. Urayoán told Diego that he could expect a large group of young Indian women to be waiting for him at the nearby Guaorabo River in order to 'satisfy his needs'. He enthusiastically agreed to be carried to the river on the shoulders of the warriors.

What happened at the river was not recorded by the Taíno. A popular theory in Puerto Rico is that when Diego Salcedo reached the river, the warriors 'accidentally' dropped him in the water and sat on his chest until he stopped moving. Even after an hour underwater, the Indians were not completely convinced that Diego was dead. Everyone knows that gods are jokers. The Indians brought his lifeless body back to the village and laid him on a comfortable straw mat and waited for him to come back to life. Even the renowned patience of the Taíno Indians had its limits. After three days in the tropical sun, Diego Salcedo was not making any progress back to the land of the living.

The Taíno were left with the conclusion that the Spaniards had pulled a fast one. They weren't gods after all. This powerful piece of knowledge proved extremely dangerous for both the Taíno and the Spaniards. When Ponce de Leon received word that the Indians had killed Diego Salcedo, he dispatched soldiers to round up the usual suspects. Six thousand Taíno were unceremoniously slaughtered. The Taíno responded. They engaged the Spaniards in guerrilla warfare for eight years. The statue of Agüeybaná II, 'El Bravo' stands proudly in the Puerto

Rican city of Ponce. It is a tribute to the man brave enough to fight the gods.

Although the conquistadors lacked many of the subtle nuances of proper gods, they did have superior firepower. The bloody eight year war between the Taíno and Spanish conquistadors proved one-sided. By the year 1520, the Taíno were hunted down and killed to near extinction in Puerto Rico. In the end, the Taíno proved to be more resilient than the conquistadors could possibly have imagined. After nearly being wiped out by the Spanish in the 16th century, their numbers have increased significantly in Puerto Rico. Today the Taíno culture is a vibrant part of Puerto Rican history. Their traditions are remembered through vocabulary, music, customs, and beliefs. According to a study by the U.S. National Science Foundation, 61% of all Puerto Ricans have Amerindian (Taíno) DNA. Puerto Ricans are Indians mixed with Africans and Europeans. When the results of this genetic study were first released, it drew tremendous criticism from the people of Puerto Rico. They first bristled at being identified as Indians. More recently, Puerto Ricans have begun to accept their heritage. Today the descendants of the Taíno are waking to their Indian past.

The relative political stability that Puerto Rico enjoys today was hard earned through the sacrifice of many brave people. In a gesture of Christian kindness after the Taíno population was almost obliterated by disease, starvation and very angry conquistadors, King Charles of Spain issued a royal decree emancipating the remaining Taíno population. With the Taíno problem neutralized, it was time to find another unwilling population to toil in the sugar cane fields. Bring on the African slaves! African slaves proved more resilient to disease, starvation, hot branding, corporal punishment and back breaking labor than the native Taíno. To the delight of the clergy, the slaves also took a shine to Christianity.

With the slaves doing most of the heavy lifting, Puerto Rico became a powerhouse in the New World. No party lasts forever. The yields from the gold mines began to dwindle around the same time that agriculture in other parts of the New World began to flourish. Competition in the Americas took much of the luster from the thriving agriculture and commercial enterprises in Puerto Rico. Even as the conquistadors' fortunes waned in Puerto Rico, the island remained an important military stronghold in the Caribbean.

The final blow to the nasty business of slavery occurred in the late 1800's after a long protracted civil uprising between the black Africans and their European hosts. The slaves were finally emancipated. With slavery abolished, the Spanish Crown needed yet another supply of cheap labor. The Royal Decree of Graces of 1815 was revived. It granted land and property rights to all Europeans willing to take residence in Puerto Rico. Prosperity prevailed and the island remained a Spanish possession until the Spanish-American war. The war ended on July 25, 1898. The Spanish Crown ceded Puerto Rico to the United States government.

The partnership between Puerto Rico and the US was tentative and unpredictable for many years. Revolts by the Puerto Rican Nationalist Party in the 1950's added greatly to the animosity between Americans and Puerto Ricans. The revolts also solidified the Puerto Ricans' resolve for more say in their future. Today Puerto Rico is an unincorporated territory of the United States. Its people are citizens of the US; they are subject to US law, but they can not vote in US elections.

Puerto Ricans fly the US flag, receive dependable mail delivery from the United States Postal Service and even have a Budweiser brewery. Plenty of mass-produced lager and American television has not managed to subdue the Puerto Ricans yearnings for statehood. A non-binding plebiscite in 2012 indicated that a majority (54%) of the Puerto Rican people favored full statehood. The one pro-independence group on the island received 5% of the vote. Five hundred years of political and military unrest did little to bring permanent stability to the island. Today, Puerto Rico is in the midst of social, economic, and political upheavals. Their unemployment rate has been stuck at double digits for decades. The island loses 15,000 people, 1.5% of its population a year, to emigration. While the young and the educated leave, the island's population becomes older and poorer. More than half of all Puerto Ricans live in New York. Puerto Rico is a very large, crowded island in a big open sea. It is an island of cultural diversity and tremendous population density. The Puerto Ricans are a friendly and laid back people always willing to help a stranger.

During all of our travels to Puerto Rico, we were universally greeted with kindness and open arms. It is a very

Quest for the Virgins

friendly place. Many people who first visit the island are struck by the cultural differences between the clichéd image of a Puerto Rican living in New York and a Puerto Rican who has never left their island home. The Puerto Ricans on the island were always quick to help us distinguish between themselves and their brothers and sisters in New York. New York is a place of opportunity for Puerto Ricans. New York is a fast and unforgiving city that requires immigrants to adapt quickly. There are differences between a resident of Puerto Rico and their counterpart in New York.

Before ever buying Quest, Wendy and I had occasion to witness this cultural morphing on flights from JFK International Airport in New York to San Juan, Puerto Rico. The first time we flew to San Juan, the plane was booked to capacity with non-tourists. It was a cross section of all ages, from children to old grandmas. In between the children and old folks were a high percentage of young men and women who had made the transition from countrified island dweller to New York gang banger. These stylish and expressive youth sported excessive displays of tasteless gold jewelry, doo rags, tattoos, brand name sneakers, tank-tops and low-slung shorts. Most importantly they had 'attitude'. We boarded the flight with rival groups flashing gang signs and displaying mildly threatening gestures.

To our surprise and relief as the non-stop flight grew closer to our destination, the general mood of the plane changed from a cabin on the brink of tribal warfare to one of only mild disgust. When the plane was approximately an hour from Luis Muñoz Marín

It's My Island Now

International Airport in San Juan, a beautiful stewardess announced that the pilot would soon begin the approach. The stewardess hadn't clipped the mike on the wall before every gang banger jumped out of their seat with a plastic shopping bag in his hand. The first piece of essential New York street apparel to be removed and placed in the bag was the two hundred pounds of heavy gold chains and 'bling'. Then out came the oxford button-down short-sleeve shirts which were put on over the tight tank-top tees. The low-slung shorts were pulled up and covered with chinos. The sneakers were replaced with shiny leather. The transition from gang banger to choir boy was smooth and seamless. While departing the plane, the young men that seemed totally at odds with each other in the waiting area of JFK were at ease and friendly in each others company in the San Juan Airport. Wendy and I were very pleased to see how the enchanted island of Puerto Rico can trump 'a New York state of mind' in a heartbeat.

Seven

Bioluminescent Bay

The thought of cruising the world's oceans on a sailboat can easily capture the imagination. For the wishful sailor, the sea is a wet and slippery path. Raise the imaginary sails and you will be carried away to your dream destination. But challenging an unforgiving ocean and testing your strength is an adventure. Wandering the world in search of your dreams is freedom.

Setting the sails is the easy part. Storms pass, followed by calms, then more storms. Acquiring the requisite skills to be a safe ocean sailor can be accomplished by any willing novice. Becoming a sailor is a good first step in the journey of discovery. For those living a contented existence contained by convention, there is little need to be troubled by freedom. For the happily discontented members of our society, escapism is abundantly supplied by the purveyors of dreams. For many of us, escapism is a powerful opiate to the constraints of 'our brave new world'.

Every sort of quick and convenient escape is marketed and sold like patent medicine. Escape is safe, convenient and time saving.

For the armchair dreamer, the thought of sailing the ocean seas evokes the ultimate notion of freedom. For the lucky few who are content to simply indulge in escape, freedom remains safely at arms length. Freedom can be a hard won reward for those brave enough to shun convention. The sailing life is a wondrous journey bounded only by the imagination. Joy is to be found in this limitless journey. Wendy and I have been very fortunate to have taken this path of discovery and freedom. Quest did a miraculous job of transporting us to a magical state of personal freedom. She helped open our eyes and point us on the right course. Freedom from convention begins this most frightening journey with the knowledge that you may become who you want to be.

The south coast of Puerto Rico has a multitude of beautiful anchorages, each with its own unique landforms and biodiversity. For boaters seeking solitude and nature, the south shore is a dream come true. The south shore anchorages are not crowded. They don't provide much allure for winter cruisers on a time schedule or the Virgin Islands charter fleet. These individuals seek a boating experience in the safety of numbers among mooring balls, burger joints and bars.

The quick sail from Boquerón to La Parguera was a short trip on a windy coastline. Within two hours of picking up the anchor in Boquerón, we were threading our way through the myriad of reefs that protect the anchorage of La Parguera. La Parguera is a fishing village and seaside retreat for Puerto Rican city dwellers. It does not attract international tourists en masse. Due to its remoteness, La Parguera retains the charm of a small community filled with real people living real lives. As we approached from the ocean, the village was hidden by reefs and islands that stretch across the harbor. Following an accurate set of waypoints, we passed though a mile long archipelago of tiny mangrove-covered islands that are barely above sea level. After clearing the outer line of reef islands, we motored through the second set of reefs and found good holding close to the city.

La Parguera is an out-of-the-way place on a large Caribbean island. A drive to the village from anywhere in Puerto Rico is an exercise in patience. Depending on how badly you get lost, it can take anywhere from two to four hours to drive from the capital of San Juan. In more recent years La Parguera has made the transition from fishing village to seaside resort. The floating cottages and houseboats that crowd the waterfront add a casual air of leisure. The wooden fishing pirogues festooned with bright oranges, blues and whites that once crowded the shoreline are slowly being displaced by whiter-than-white plastic v-hulls. The common fisherman's way of life is giving way to the lucrative sport fishing industry. It was very interesting to sail into La Parguera and see the new and the old. Puerto Rico is a very populous island where contrasts are commonplace. There are few places in the world where you will find a fisherman's shack and a wooden pirogue right beside a floating mansion and a $400,000 sport fishing boat. The issues associated with extreme income disparity were not obvious. La Parguera is definitely a laid back place on a laid back island.

We had arrived and were happily swinging at anchor before ten in the morning. With the sails stowed and the dinghy lowered, we were off to pick up a very large bundle of mail which Wendy had forwarded to the local Post Office. Many full-time cruisers who do not have a permanent address use a mail forwarding service in their home country. This mail service is commonly known as a Commercial Mail Receiving Agency (CMRA). A CMRA is registered with the US Postal Service and is tasked with receiving private mail for the purpose of collection and redelivery. For an extra fee CMRA's will open, digitally scan the mail and send it to their clients via email. Wendy had called our CMRA in South Florida when we were in Boquerón. After several months of cruising, our mail bag had begun to bulge into an unwieldy bundle. On Wendy's call, they packed the letters in a box and sent it to the La Parguera Post office.

Motoring up to the waterfront was a treat for the eyes. Flamboyantly decorated houses painted in fluorescent shades of purple, blue, yellow and green were erected on pilings that crowded the shoreline and impinged on the mangroves. It was a quiet Wednesday morning. Only a handful of locals were scattered among the small downtown shops. The bars and restaurants occupied prime real estate. They had yet to open their doors for the day's business.

Quest for the Virgins

La Parguera is a pleasant enough small, sleepy seaside resort. We found the Post Office easily.

"This is a big pile of mail. You should go home more often" the woman at the Post Office said to Wendy.

"We are home. Our house is out there" Wendy said pointing in the direction of the bay.

"Oh, you live on a boat" she said with a big broad smile. "What's it like living on a boat?"

"It's a great way to see the Caribbean without paying for planes, hotels and restaurants" Wendy replied.

The lady nodded and smiled. I gave Wendy a light tap in the middle of the back and whispered in her ear "Let's get going."

Wendy looked at the clerk and said "Living on a boat is great."

We strode the empty streets and passed wall to wall restaurants. We perused every menu for vegetarian entrees.

"Do you see something you like?" I asked.

"I think a little Italian would be nice" she said.

We walked back to the Italian restaurant and studied the bill of fare.

"We still have some mushrooms that we bought in Boquerón and a little Romano cheese. Could you make this fettuccini in a creamy porcini sauce?" she said.

"Two orders of fettuccini alfredo it will be" I said.

We turned and headed back to Quest before the party-goers had a chance to wake.

At the stroke of eleven, the tourists began to mill about the village looking for their first meal of the day. In the galley, I gathered the ingredients for the alfredo sauce while Wendy sat in the cockpit watching the tourists with binoculars. The galley in a Bayfield 36 or any cruising boat has more than enough space and equipment to prepare a gourmet five-course meal. It does take a bit of compromise. The most essential piece of equipment in any small galley is the ability to improvise.

Button mushrooms are a distant, blander cousin of the porcini. A good way to approximate a porcini is to gently fry about a half pound of finely sliced button mushrooms in a pat of butter. When the mushrooms begin to wilt, add a pinch of oregano and dried basil. Continue frying until they just begin to brown. Add a half clove of super-thin garlic slices and a pinch of onion powder. When the garlic is translucent, deglaze the pan with a half cup of a good white wine and a quarter teaspoon of tamari (soy sauce). Reduce the heat and poach for about fifteen minutes. When the pan is almost dry, add a tablespoon of butter and a teaspoon of white flour. Cook the flour until it is just beginning to brown. Remove the pan from the heat and add the cream. I didn't have any 'half and half'. I did have the old standby, canned non-sweetened condensed milk. I added a quarter of a can of evaporated milk and the same amount of water and stirred it with the roux to thicken. A few teaspoons of Romano cheese and a pinch of pepper finished off the sauce.

While I boiled the fettuccini, Wendy gave me a running commentary on the fleet of sport fishing boats.

"They've started their engines and are pulling up to the starting line" Wendy quipped.

As I carried the two plates of fettucini to the cockpit, the over-crowded sport fishing boats whipped by in single formation.

"It looks like 'Mucho Dinero' is in the poll position with 'Little Fish' coming up close in second. 'La Gorda Albóndigus' is bringing up the rear as you would expect."

When the fleet had finally passed and their wakes were slapping the other end of the anchorage, I placed the 'Pasta Fungi e Latte Evaporata' on the cockpit table with a half bottle of cheap chardonnay. After a few minutes, the stink of the outboards had drifted a sufficient distance for us to be able to enjoy our food. It was a great meal in a most wonderful location. Wendy picked up the binoculars and looked at the Italian restaurant suspended over the shoreline on pilings.

"Look" she said. "Right at the end of the veranda. Do you see the woman with the red blouse? She's eating fettuccini in a creamy porcini sauce" she said with a grin.

She handed me the binoculars.

"The woman in the red blouse is eating a bread stick" I said.

"Oh yeah? Give me those binoculars."

We spent the rest of the day in pleasant, tropical idle pursuits. The fishing fleet returned at sundown and churned the anchorage as they docked their boats. The village came alive after sundown. The brightly lighted strings of Christmas bulbs that hung in every archway sparkled off the calm waters of the anchorage. We took pleasure in hearing the sounds of music and merriment drift across the anchorage. At midnight the village went dark and silent in a half hour as the sidewalks were rolled up.

As we went to bed, I had no idea that our floor show was just about to begin. Around two o'clock in the morning, I climbed in the cockpit and looked around the anchored boats for anyone still awake in their cockpits. Everything was quiet. I walked to the bow and proceeded to pee over the bow pulpit. When the stream hit the water, it came to life with a bright, bluish green, sparkly brilliance. In a half conscious state, I stared at the water mesmerized. 'So this is what bioluminescence looks like' I thought. Both Wendy and I had infrequently seen bioluminescence at sea. Occasionally on night sails when the bow strikes a large head sea, the wave would instantly flash with this same blue green light. Then the illuminated water would streak down both sides of the hull, meet at the stern and disappear in our wake. Bioluminescence is much different while at anchor. It takes some getting used to and it never gets ordinary.

Many life forms have the ability to produce light. In the far majority of light-emitting organisms, the light is produced by biochemistry or a chemiluminescence reaction. The firefly is an example of a garden variety luminescent life form. Even fungus and bacteria can emit light. The marine organisms that were glowing in La Parguera were the dinoflagellates or what Wendy and I began to humorously refer to as 'dinoflashlights'. Dinoflagellates are single-celled algae called phytoplankton. La Parguera's location, tides and indigenous marine growth encourage an abundance of bioluminescence.

Wendy and I had never seen bioluminescence in an anchorage. I crept down the companionway stairs and eagerly woke her. She reached for the light.

"Don't turn the light on" I said.

"What's going on? It's two in the morning" she said.

"Follow me" I said. I led her to the foredeck. "Sit down" I said motioning to the cabin top.

"What's up?" she asked.

"You're not going to believe this" I said.

I extended the boat hook to its maximum length.

"Watch the water real close" I said.

I touched the surface of the water with the tip of the boat hook. A brilliant aquamarine dot appeared in the darkness. It radiated rings of light. Wendy stepped to the rail.

"What is it?" she asked.

"Bioluminescence" I said.

"That has to be the coolest thing I have ever seen" she said.

I made a long arc in the water with the boot hook.

"It looks like Tinker Bell and her wand" Wendy said with glee.

"What do you say to a night dip? Let me dive in first, so you can see when I break the surface" I said.

I pulled off my shorts, arched above the railing and plunged in. Just after I broke the surface, I opened my eyes. The water around me flashed. I came to the surface and floated on my back. In the background I could hear Wendy jumping up and down on the deck. I looked at my chest. The luminescence surrounded me like a luminous skin.

"Jump in, the water's warm" I said.

Wendy jumped in. The area surrounding us glowed with an eerie blue light. We treaded water for about five minutes. Every time we churned the water with our arms, we turned on more dinoflashlights. Our antics were enough to wake the crew of an adjacent boat.

"What's going on out there?" came a voice from the darkness.

"He'll go away" I whispered to Wendy.

"OK, who's out there? What do you want?" the man repeated in a low, unpleasant tone.

"It's David and Wendy from Quest" I said.

"What's going on? It's two o'clock. Is your boat sinking?" he asked.

"No, everything's OK. It's the bioluminescence. It's spectacular tonight" I said.

"Is that all? First timers, you woke up the whole anchorage over that?" he shouted.

"Take it easy. Let's call it a night" I said.

I watched as the luminescence clung to Wendy's body as she climbed the stern ladder. I looked over at our neighbor who was also enjoying the view.

I shouted over to his boat "Hey, go back to bed."

Eight

The Jet Ski Cometh

Our brief stop in La Parguera provided us with both a rare glimpse into the magical world of bioluminescence and our first sighting of an authentic native Puerto Rican tourist. Despite the allure of night swimming with two billion glowing dinoflagellates, it was time to jump back into the trade winds and brave a two hour sail. After passing the coastal industrial town of Guanica and the large Copamarina Beach Resort, we took shelter behind a group of low islands called Cayos de Caña Gorda. For lack of a more creative alternative, Cayos de Caña Gorda is referred to as Gilligan's Island by the locals.

The anchorage was completely deserted and peaceful when we set the hook at ten in the morning. All semblance of tranquility would soon disappear. It was a high pitched whine that first interrupted our noon day meal of salad and warm bread.

"What's that noise?" Wendy asked as she passed me the plate of black olives and feta cheese. "It sounds like a swarm of bees."

"I have a funny feeling that this is going to be worse than a bee sting" I replied.

The sound grew louder and more defined.

"We are about to be overrun" I said as five Jet Skis whipped around the point of land separating the resort from the anchorage.

The tight formation of buzzing machines changed a peaceful natural experience into an adrenaline overload. When the flotilla of five Jet Skis first entered the anchorage, they seemed content to tear up the shore line, erode the mangrove roots and frighten off the bird life. Quest was anchored in about fifteen feet of water, dead-center in the small bay. After twenty minutes of mindless destruction, three of the Jet Skiers took their craft into the ocean to jump the big waves. This left two riders. Two Jet Skis were plenty to take the luster off our paradise.

Jet Skis are one of the most ubiquitous small personal watercraft in the world. With a draft of only a few inches, they can be operated very close to shore. They accelerate extremely fast and can attain speeds of over fifty miles per hour. The operator of a Jet Ski does not require a license yet they are subject to all the rules that govern the operation of a forty foot boat. They are among the noisiest of all watercraft. A big muscle Jet Ski can consume 24 gallons of gasoline per hour.

In brief, this class of boat is extremely popular. They burn inordinate amounts of petrochemicals for their size. The engine design allows unburned gasoline to run out of the exhaust and into the water. The noise pollution is loud and offensive. When Jet Skis are operated in a safe and reasonable manner, they are still big polluters. Their unmuffled engines are a nuisance. They cause billions of dollars in damage to shorelines. If they are operated by the inexperienced and careless, they are very dangerous machines. Reckless driving, drunk driving, inexperience and excessive speeding exact a heavy toll in death and injury. These consequences do little to dampen the public's enthusiasm.

After the three men on Jet Skis left the anchorage, the two remaining women became increasingly emboldened with their shiny toys. One of the women, slim and petite, was very timid on her machine. She kept to a moderate speed and made all attempts to drive in a careful manner. Her girlfriend, who was wearing a two piece bikini, could well have tipped the scales at 300 pounds. Her generous girth pushed the back of the Jet Ski into the water. She did not demonstrate the same concern for safety and good manners that her girlfriend did. As the anchorage became more and more filled with gasoline fumes, the stout woman became very reckless. She seemed happy to randomly zip about the anchorage with abandon. Within twenty minutes the pair tired of doing figure eights. They now sought serious and advanced recklessness. Thus far the pair of riders had barely glanced at Quest.

Wendy and I both saw it coming. They stopped and drifted about 100 yards from Quest.

"Why are they pointing over here? What do you think they want?" Wendy asked.

"It's probably nothing. They're probably ready to hit us up for a cold beer" I said.

87

We watched in disbelief as the large woman gunned her Jet Ski and accelerated towards Quest. She temporarily lost equilibrium when the machine's acceleration pushed her back on the seat. After she regained her balance, she raced directly at Quest and sped ten feet past the stern.

"Is she crazy?" Wendy yelled over the noise of the engine. The corpulent woman spun her ride around and made her next high speed pass directly at the bow, coming inches away from the anchor chain.

"If she hits the chain going that fast, it's going to be one big crash" I said.

I raced to the bow just as she started to make the next pass.

"How do you say chain in Spanish?" I yelled to Wendy.

"Try cadena, or just point and yell anything!" she said over the sound of the Jet Ski.

As the woman made her approach, I waved my hands then pointed to the anchor chain and yelled "CATARINA!"

As she passed dangerously close, she threw back her head and roared a frightening cackle of laughter. Adding tremendously to the drama of the moment was her glassy-eyed drunk look. I walked back to the cockpit as she began her turn to pass astern.

"We've got a problem" I said. "She definitely looks DUI."

"Drunk at eleven o'clock. Party down!" Wendy laughed.

Emboldened by her close passes on the bow and

the stern, she began to do a series of fifty foot rings around Quest. On every pass she came closer and closer. As the wave energy compounded, Quest began to rock. Wendy and I held on to the cockpit combing.

"She's eventually going to run out of gas" I said.

What was this woman thinking? Was she thinking? From fifty feet away, she seemed possessed by a primitive force bent on destruction and anger. I'm glad I wasn't her next door neighbor. Around and around she went. On each pass she kept up a constant maniacal laugh. Quest pitched from side to side. The air was turning blue from fumes and the water developed the purple-green sheen of unburned petroleum.

"There is one thing that we can do" I said confidently. "Get into your bathing suit. This is an excellent time to clean the waterline."

After climbing into the dinghy with our brushes, Wendy held onto Quest's toe rail as I began to clean the grime from the waterline. The woman continued to circle. On each pass we did our best to demonstrate our disapproval of her inconsiderate behavior.

Then the moment finally arrived that helped restore sanity. After a particularly reckless turn, the Jet Ski abruptly toppled to the right and ejected her. The engine stalled. The driverless machine drifted for a few feet. The woman's girlfriend slowly motored over and offered the woman her hand. Wendy and I immediately grabbed the dinghy oars and paddled over to retrieve the Jet Ski. If we got her back in the saddle she might leave us alone for the rest of the day. When we pulled the Jet Ski close enough, she grabbed on in desperation. She was quite scared and disoriented but showed no outward sign of injury. Her girlfriend wasn't holding up much better. For what good it did, I tried to calm the hysterical friend.

"Tell her to calm down" I said to Wendy.

"Cállate" Wendy said emphatically.

That made the pair even more wild eyed.

"What did you say?"

"I said shut up."

"Don't say that anymore."

The girlfriend was a write-off.

"I think we just volunteered" I said to Wendy. "Ask 'her largeness' if she can ride."

"Puedes montar?"

"Sí" she mumbled.

I jumped into the water and tried to push her back onto the Jet Ski. I didn't move her an inch.

"Come on you two" I said to Wendy and the girlfriend. "Give me a hand here."

The three of us struggled, pushed and pulled. The woman was so well-oiled and greased up with suntan lotion that she slid off every time we made any progress. We needed to bring in the reserves.

"Tell her friend to go back to the resort for help" I said.

Wendy looked at the girlfriend and said very slowly "Obtener ayuda."

"No, no, I can't. I stay here!" she mumbled in Spanglish.

"Someone has to go to the resort and get help" I

said. "We can't just leave her here. I've got an idea. Let's see if we can get her over to Quest's stern."

"Why?" Wendy said.

"It's worth a try. I'm going to see if we can pick her up with the lifesling on the dinghy davits."

Wendy temporarily lost her composure and laughed. "Can the davits handle that kind of bulk?" she said.

"Probably. We'll know when they bend or break" I said. "I'd ask her to climb the swim ladder but I think she would pull it right off the boat."

As the desperate woman held onto the Jet Ski, we maneuvered her under the dinghy davits.

"Tell your girlfriend that I am going on board to get the lifesling."

The girlfriend shrugged, looked at the bedraggled woman and translated. I climbed into the cockpit and slipped the lifesling out of its rack on the stern pulpit.

"Put her shoulders in here" I said to Wendy and the girlfriend.

"Do you have the lifesling enlarging tool?" Wendy said.

"Just try it" I said.

91

They slipped her hands into the harness and it immediately became stuck at her elbows.

"Forget it. It's never going to fit" I said.

I then retrieved a length of ¾ inch nylon line from the starboard winch locker. Forming a large harness out of a bowline knot, I attached it to the davit tackle.

"Slip this over her head and under her armpits" I said handing Wendy the harness.

"Where are they?" she said.

"Where's what?" I said.

"Her armpits."

I turned around to suppress a laugh. "They're probably somewhere in the fleshy area somewhere below her shoulders. Just make sure that you put the sling above the bikini top. We don't want anything to break loose there" I said.

Wendy and the girlfriend enlarged the rope sling and slipped it over the obese woman's head and under their best guess at her shoulders. After pulling the slack out of the block and tackle, I started to heave on the line. She came out of the water about three inches. Then the line slipped through my fingers.

"Tell your girlfriend to hold on. I'm going to try something" I said hopefully.

Wrapping the line around a winch drum, I began cranking on the winch handle. The line went taut and inch by inch she came out of the water.

"Stop, stop" Wendy said as the woman began to cry out in pain.

I lowered her back into the water where she held

onto the Jet Ski in panic. I ran to the stern.

"What's going on?"

"This isn't working. What's plan B, Professor?"

"Plan B? Well, plan B is to get three big guys from the resort to get her back onto the Jet Ski."

The resort was about a mile by water. It could take hours to get help.

"Let me see if I can raise them with the hand-held radio. I don't know what the range of this thing is, but I'll try" I said as I powered up the VHF.

"Come in Copamarina Beach Resort. This is Quest" I said into the microphone.

"Quest. Quest who?" came back the reply in a distinct British accent.

"This is the Sailing vessel Quest, over."

"This is Jesse. I'm anchored in Guanica. I'm in the restaurant having lunch. What's up?"

"Can you get the resort manager?"

"Sure, he's sitting at the table with me."

A moment later the resort manager took the mic. "How can I help you? You wish to make reservations?"

"No, there is a problem with one of your guests in the anchorage east of the resort."

"A Jet Ski problem?" he asked. I looked over at Wendy. "If one of our guests is driving recklessly, I apologize. There isn't much I can do."

"No" I said. "One of your guests has fallen off their Jet Ski and they can't get back on."

"OK, I send over a big boy to help."

"You're going to need more than a big boy. There

are three of us and we can't budge her" I said.

There was a pause. "Oh, I think that I saw the guest that you are talking about leave from the beach. Is she hurt?"

"No, not that I can tell. I would suggest sending over at least two of your strongest men."

"I will send them right over and thank you for your help" he replied.

Within fifteen minutes two body builder types came racing into the anchorage in a Zodiac. They seemed completely confused and somewhat amused when they saw the woman hanging from the dinghy davit crane.

"Hola, hola" said the leader of the rescue party. "It looks like you caught yourself a big one today" he said in extremely good English.

"Yes" I said embarrassed.

"When the sling is removed, we'll have her out of here in a minute" he said.

Wendy looked at the girlfriend and said "You first."

The line was somewhat hidden by adipose tissue. After a bit of struggling, the girlfriend freed the knot and pulled the line over her head.

The young man looked at me with machismo and said "We'll take over now."

The two men jumped in the water and began pushing on the woman's ample bottom. After a couple of minutes they were exhausted.

"She's a slippery one" he said. "Sir, could we possibly use your dinghy paddles?"

"Sure" I said.

The Jet Ski Cometh

Wendy handed each man a paddle. They each placed a paddle under the woman's bottom while they caught the flat tip of the paddle on each side of the Jet Ski. With both of the men working together they managed to leverage her up onto the seat with brute force.

"Where did you learn that trick?" I asked.

"We never had to go to this extreme with a guest. We have a problem similar to this from time to time" he said with a smile.

"How's that?" I asked.

"Sometimes a frozen side of beef falls off the delivery truck. If we can't get enough people to help, we have to use a couple steel pipes to pry the carcass back onto the handcart."

He reached over and shook my hand. "I really want to thank you" he said. "Normally when we get called over here we have to deal with some real angry boaters." He had just pushed off Quest's rail when he turned around. "I almost forgot" he said reaching into the Zodiac. "The manager wanted you to have this."

He handed me a large Ziploc bag with the restaurant's menu inside.

"Thanks" I said, a bit surprised.

He tied the Jet Ski's painter to the stern of the Zodiac and slowly motored out of the anchorage with one humiliated guest in tow. When the resort crew had left the anchorage with their charges, I opened the Ziploc.

"Take a look at this" I said to Wendy.

"Wow" she said. "This is a pretty upscale restaurant. There's not much here for vegetarians."

"At these prices would you expect anything vegetarian?" I said.

"Not really."

A half hour later we heard a call on the VHF.

"Quest, come in. This is the manager of the resort."

"This is Quest" I said.

He profusely apologized for the problem that his guest had caused us.

"I would like to invite you and your lovely wife to have dinner at the resort's restaurant" he said.

"That's a very kind offer" I said. "We'll get back to you."

"OK, anytime" he replied.

Nine

The Porta-Potty

Motoring to the resort to accept the manager's gracious offer was sidetracked as the anchorage returned to a place of quiet and solitude. Floating gently at anchor and completely alone in the mangroves at Cayos de Caña Gorda was not an experience that could be replaced by an upscale Surf and Turf restaurant.

"We missed a good 'all you can eat' meal" Wendy said as I plated the couscous and grilled vegetables.

"What are you talking about?" I said.

"Hey if we'd gone to the restaurant they would have treated us like heroes" she said.

"That's what I was afraid of. Picture this, we land on the beach in front of the restaurant. A restaurant overflowing with smiling patrons stand to attention. Throngs of admirers rush towards us. They hoist the two of us on their shoulders. Small children scatter flower petals as we are carried into the restaurant amid the joyous chorus of 'they saved La Gorda'. We are ceremoniously lowered from their shoulders where we find ourselves literally smothered in embraces from our Jet Ski antagonist. Then the head chef and the two body builders strain under the weight of the house specialty, a whole roasted pig wrapped up inside a barbecued cow. The grand dame of personal watercraft brandishes a razor sharp machete and slices it in half and presents it to us. "Eat" she says throwing her head back cackling in her all too familiar maniacal laugh."

"Sounds good" Wendy said. "Do you think that they would have a decent Cabernet to go with the entree?"

"In my story, only the giant cow-pig 'Twinkie' is part of the all you can eat. The Cheval Blanc 1947 is billed separately."

By eight o'clock we were both winding down from a day rudely interrupted by our life saving duties. We were weary. I retired for the day, considering the possibility that maybe one person, besides me, had learned a memorable lesson about safety on small watercraft.

Having knowledge of the future is an attribute that most Wall Street bond traders would gladly give their right hand for. As a sailor, I am always glad that the future is uncertain. I feel lucky that I can't tell the future. If I could, I would be too afraid to leave the harbor. I was happy to have no foreknowledge of our next sail. It would be Wendy's day to be brave.

Quest's bow had barely cleared the protection of the Cayos de Caña Gorda when we were hit by the force of the trades. The onshore wind conditions created a lee shore. We were only making a ten mile hop. I pointed Quest into the wind and raised the main. The wind would be against us for three hours. Our final destination of the day was Isla Caja de Muertos, a small island eight miles off the south coast of Puerto Rico. But first we needed to make a brief stop in the busy port town of Ponce to take on diesel fuel.

The decision to tow the dinghy that day created a problem. The powerful trade wind and currents were generating a rough sea state. As we sailed further offshore, the dinghy was thrown about like a leaf. Then it started to take on water at an alarming rate. My first attempt to remedy the situation was to pull in on the painter and bring the dinghy close into the lee of Quest's stern. Due to the style and design of our dinghy, this made matters worse. Two years before we had chosen a plastic folding dinghy to accompany us on our travels to the Caribbean. It was composed of a number of folding plastic panels that can be collapsed into a shape resembling a surf board. Although the description may sound a bit wacky, it was actually an extremely fit small craft. It was also so light that it could be carried under the arm. The combination of the bullet proof Mylar, weight and fold-ability gave it tremendous advantages over a conventional inflatable dinghy. The only single disadvantage of the ultra lightweight design was its instability while being towed in heavy seas.

As we watched the dinghy flail about in our wake, it continued to take on water. In minutes it would be in jeopardy of swamping. As we pushed further offshore, the waves built into a confusing mess of pyramidal tops. I wasn't looking forward to the nasty job of climbing down the swim ladder, bailing out a hundred gallons of salt water, then attaching the dinghy to the davit cranes. If Wendy could keep the bow of Quest perfectly straight, it wouldn't be too bad in the calm behind the boat.

"You have to keep Quest on a dead straight course while I climb into the dinghy."

"The sea is too rough. I'll never keep us straight."

"Do you want to go fix the dinghy?" I asked.

"No way. How straight do I have to keep her?" Wendy said.

"Straight enough that I'll always stay in Quest's wake" I said handing Wendy the wheel.

Wendy possessed very limited ability to steer anything in a straight line.

"The waves are coming from everywhere. Look out front and compensate when you see a big wave coming for the bow" I said.

I watched in desperation as Wendy struggled and strained with the helm. Nobody's perfect. Every transient gust and big wave sent the bow of Quest jerking from port to starboard. After a couple of minutes of watching the bow dodge back and forth, I completely lost patience.

"We don't have time for you to learn to steer. We have to do something right now."

I could tell that Wendy knew what was coming next. Her eyes went glassy and she started to wipe her palms on her tee shirt.

Before she completely shrank away I said "We're in a tough spot here. I have the option of cutting the dinghy free or sending you into the dinghy while I steer Quest."

She started to back away. This defining moment required an inspirational theme.

"YOU'RE going to save the dinghy" I said.

"No way baby. I'm not going out there. Cut it loose. We can buy another ugly dinghy."

"Everything is going to be all right" I said in a calm voice.

"You've got to be kidding. Everything is going to be all right? That didn't even work for Bob Marley. Get him to save the dinghy."

I needed to be a little more persuasive.

"It's pretty safe. You just have to work quick" I said.

"Safe, are you nuts?"

She wasn't quite convinced. I reached into the cockpit locker and worked fast.

"Here's you safety harness" I said pulling it from the locker. "Turn around." Fitting the harness around her torso, I cinched the strap tight.

"OK, I'm going to attach the tether. Turn around again."

Taking the end of a thirty foot length of heavy nylon line, I tied a bowline knot through the two rings on the harness.

"You're going to do great" I said. "Hold onto the transom until I get Quest sailing dead straight. I'll give you the signal."

I turned around and grabbed the wheel. After a couple of seconds Quest was making a straight line through the heavy seas.

"OK, start pulling the dinghy towards Quest until

it's practically touching the stern and don't get in until I say."

Strapping on the safety harness had calmed Wendy down considerably. When she had the dinghy pulled in, I put two wraps of the safety tether around a starboard winch drum.

As a wave began to lift the dinghy, I shouted "Go."

I let the tether slowly slip around the drum with my right hand, cleated the dinghy painter to the transom and held onto the wheel with my left. Wendy can be agile when she needs to be. She was over the stern rail and into the dinghy before I had a chance to blink.

"Take this" I said throwing her a bailing bucket.

She was doing very well. When a large quantity of water was bailed from the dinghy, I turned to the stern and saw the dinghy motor flopping about in the breakers.

"Secure that dinghy engine" I shouted over the wind.

"How?"

"Tighten the big wing nut at the front of the motor housing."

Wendy slid to the stern of the dinghy and started to loosen the nut.

"The other way. Turn the wing nut the other way" I yelled.

With the motor secured, half the problem was solved.

"Get back on board. Leave the bucket in the dinghy" I said.

There was no way that we could possibly raise the

dinghy onto the davits in these seas. As Wendy scurried up the stern ladder, I attached the dinghy painter to the starboard davit and hauled up until the bow was two feet out of the water. Wendy jumped into the cockpit in jubilation and began to do a victory dance around the steering wheel.

With her hands over her head she jumped about chanting "I DID it! I DID it! I saved the dinghy."

Removing the safety harness I said "Sit down and take a break, hero."

"I can't sit down now, I'm too jacked-up" she shouted. "I saved the dinghy. I saved the dinghy."

The dinghy would be temporarily safe until we could make our way to the calm waters of Ponce Bay.

During our travels we constantly ran into many people who were surprised and confounded when we arrived at a dock with our folding dinghy. How we came to own such an unusual craft was due to the many disadvantages of inflatables. When we first purchased Quest, she came equipped with a practically new inflatable dinghy and a very heavy 15 horsepower motor. Within a week of moving from the landlocked city of Charlotte, North Carolina to Fernandina Beach, Florida we were eager to inflate the dinghy and slip her into the water to explore the marshes in Egan's Creek. The marshes in and about the tidal flats were a magnificent place to enjoy nature. Hundreds of species of colorful water fowl as well as small alligators, manatees, and dolphins populated the marsh. It was a marine and bird life sanctuary.

Quest for the Virgins

On a bright summer morning we put into Egan's Creek for our maiden voyage on our new inflatable. The marsh was approaching full flood tide. The tidal swing in Egan's Creek was about eight feet that day. As we passed under the fixed road bridge on 14th Street, the razor sharp barnacles and mussels on the pilings were underwater and out of sight. This was the first time that Wendy and I had been in any dinghy. It was a perfect day in the marsh. The warm morning light gave the marsh grasses a beautiful golden glow framed against the backdrop of the live oaks in distant Fort Clinch State Park.

At a safe, low rpm, we explored far up the creek and stopped for an early lunch in a small tidal tributary.

"It looks like the tide is going out pretty fast" I said to Wendy. "We better get out of here before we have to walk home."

With the tide beginning to ebb and the mud flats exposed, Egan's Creek took on a completely different character. Thousands of crabs crawled about sideways in search of tiny morsels. Majestic flocks of pelicans soared over head. Roseate spoonbills and egrets hunted in the mud flats waiting for lunch to swim by. As we drew closer to the fixed bridge, a few small alligators jumped from the banks into the channel. As we approached the bridge with the tide now at ebb, we noticed that the exposed pilings were covered with a dense growth of shells and large barnacles.

"Hey Wendy, check out the growth on those pilings. They're covered in shells."

My curiosity got the better of me. I slowed down to take a closer look. The right pontoon of the dinghy gently brushed a razor sharp cluster of mussels on the piling. Before I had time to react, the right pontoon was sliced open and deflated. The left pontoon kept us above the water long enough to make it safely to the docks of the marina. After checking with an inflatable repair shop the next day, the poor inflatable was pronounced permanently out of action.

The accidental slicing of the dinghy convinced me that I was not going to leave for the Caribbean with another inflatable. The only alternative was to equip Quest with a hard dinghy. Hard dinghies proved to be much too heavy for Wendy and me to pack around. While searching for a better alternative, I happened upon a collapsible dinghy called a Porta-Bote.

"What do you think of this boat?" I said to Wendy showing her the manufacturers web site on the screen.

"Bote, you want to buy a boat from a company that can't spell boat?"

"Who cares if they can spell boat? They mold plastic. Look, the Navy buys them" I said trying to gain some traction.

"The Navy probably buys them for target practice. That is about the ugliest thing I have ever seen" Wendy laughed.

Wendy's opposition did little to dissuade me. I ordered a ten foot Porta-bote and a 5 hp Johnson engine that day. When UPS delivered the Porta-Bote a week later, I was excited and proud as we unloaded the package.

"Cool, is this a surf board?" the young UPS driver said as we lay it on the ground.

"No this is a state-of-the-art dinghy. It's a Porta-Bote" I said with great enthusiasm. "Do you want to see it?"

"No man. I'm not into dinghies, just surfing" he said getting back into the big brown truck.

I was so proud when we carried the Porta-Bote down to the dock for its assembly and maiden voyage.

I was even sure that I had made the right decision when the grumpy marina owner walked up and said "Make sure you get this ugly piece of trash off the dock before today's race, Beaupré."

Captain K's harsh remark opened the door to the never ending litany of abuse that I would have to endure over my folding boat. The Porta-Bote was assembled and in the water with the five horsepower motor attached in less than fifteen minutes. As we cautiously pushed off the dock, one of our boat neighbors stuck his head out of his companionway.

"WOW" he said enthusiastically.

I beamed with pride. Finally I had found an aficionado of folding boats. Then the bomb shell was delivered.

"I've never seen a Porta Potty up close" he said.

"It's a Porta-Bote" I said correcting him.

"No man. Take another look. That is definitely a Porta-Potty. It looks just like half an outhouse" he said with a wink as he went back into his boat.

Somewhat deflated I laughed and steered down the Creek into the Sound. When I saw the big waves in Cumberland Sound, I started to have second thoughts about the little boat's seaworthiness.

"Let's give it a try" I said to Wendy as I gunned the small outboard.

The Porta-Bote is so light and flat that it only has a draft of a few inches and can come up on plane with only a fraction of the horsepower that an inflatable requires. The most surprising aspect was its extremely stable ride. With the engine at full throttle we literally skimmed over the waves in the Sound and reached the marshes on the other side in surprising safety. After a thoroughly safe and interesting trip, we returned to the dock a few hours later in our new purchase.

With little fanfare and a can of diet ginger ale, we christened the ugly dinghy "The Porta-Potty". It was a fitting name that stuck and one that everyone could agree upon.

The Porta-Potty served us extremely well over the years. We explored caves in the Bahamas with razor sharp coral. The dinghy also held up to shell-littered beaches that would have eaten an inflatable. After a few years in the tropical sun it became even more ugly. We never had to lock it up, even in the most theft prone anchorages. The most desperate dinghy thief wouldn't condescend to steal a Porta-Potty with a five horsepower engine.

Ten

Baja Baby

With the bow of the dinghy raised and protected from further abuse, we sailed a zigzag course eastward to take on fuel at the large port city of Ponce. Quest was equipped with a 50 gallon jumbo-sized diesel tank and a diesel fuel polishing system. The big tank allowed us tremendous freedom and flexibility on where and when we stopped for fuel. Since leaving Florida we had fueled only once in Nassau, Bahamas. I didn't want to stop just anywhere for diesel. Ponce would be an extremely opportune time.

I think it would be fair to say that most boaters give very little thought to diesel fuel. Why would anybody care? It's nasty if it splashes on anything. If you get enough diesel on your decks, it will turn them yellow. Most people want to fill their tanks and forget about it. Outside of the marine head, it is the least glamorous and least understood aspect of cruising. A simple, brief discussion with any good marine diesel mechanic may save life and boat. The overwhelming cause of diesel engine problems is bad diesel. Dirt, bacteria and water can shut an engine down in seconds. Most boaters recognize the importance of having an auxiliary engine. They are great for docking, passing through a reef on a windless day or just trying to get a few more horsepower when a big current takes hold of the boat. Sometimes it's the motor, not the sails, that keeps a boat off the rocks.

As a safety device, the auxiliary engine must start and operate flawlessly when called upon. Conversely an engine that won't start in emergencies is a disaster waiting to happen. As the captain and chief engineer, it was my responsibility to maintain an adequate level of clean diesel fuel in a clean tank.

The large ocean swell was immediately subdued as we sailed into the large and busy Bahia de Ponce. The Ponce Yacht Club was visible on a spit of land off to starboard. Dropping the main, I steered a straight course for the diesel dock. Even from a half mile away with binoculars, the fuel dock was a blur of activity. I assumed a holding pattern behind a large sport fishing boat. In less than a half hour, two dock workers caught our stern and forward lines.

"Hold on for a moment" I said to the young man handing me the fuel hose. "I need to get my Baja."

He shrugged his shoulders. He didn't seem to have a clue what I was talking about.

"It's a diesel filter" I said holding up the Baja filter.

"Papa" the young man shouted into a shack on the dock.

Baja Baby

An old sun-beaten gent rose from his chair and teetered up the dock. "¿Que?"

"Captain wants to use a filter" the young man said to his father.

The old man ran to Quest's toe rail. "No filter, too slow. You put it in there" he said pointing at the deck fill.

"What's the problem?" I said to the young man.

"He doesn't like diesel filters. I'm supposed to tell him if anyone tries to use a filter. He is very stubborn. If you argue, he won't sell you diesel. Just put the filter away. Then bring it out when he goes back in the shack."

When the old man saw me put the caps back on the Baja filter, he walked back to the fuel shack and went to sleep.

"OK, you can bring the filter out now. How does it work?" he asked.

"The Baja comes with three filters: a water filter, a coarse debris filter and a fine debris filter" I demonstrated.

"Our diesel is very clean. You won't find any problems with the fuel."

"How full are your bunker tanks?"

He looked at me quizzically. "Why do you ask?"

"The worst diesel is going to be in the last quarter of a bunker tank. That's where much of the trash settles."

"Hold on. I'll check" he said. He ran to the shack and checked the level of his tanks on a display. "Well" he said. "We haven't gotten diesel in a week and it's the weekend. They're about one third full."

"You're going to be surprised at what comes out of this hose. If you get an old newspaper I'll dump out what we collect after the fuel up" I said.

I slipped the end of the Baja into the diesel deck fitting. The second I squeezed the nozzle into the Baja filter, a small glob of black slime was captured by the first filter. After taking on 133 liters (thirty-five gallons) of fuel I handed the nozzle back.

"There aren't any boats waiting to fuel. You can stay on the dock until someone comes" he said. "I want to see what you got in the filter."

After I let the filter drain completely, I asked him if he had the newspaper.

"Sí sí" he said walking to the shack and taking the newspaper from his sleeping father's hands.

We took the filter and the newspaper over to the concrete break-wall.

"First I am going to tip it over and get the worst out."

He placed the newspaper on the concrete and I

dumped out the sediment that was caught in the filter.

"I can't believe it" he said.

There were the usual very visible black globs of bacteria and paraffin. Then I removed the three separate filters.

"Look at this" I said holding the coarse filter up to the sun.

He let out a long whistle through his closed teeth. "What is it?"

We sifted through the particles.

"This looks like sand."

"Yeah, looks like sand" I said. "Here are a few bits of rust" I said pointing to some red spots.

When the water filter was disassembled an even bigger surprise awaited him. When the water strainer was tipped onto the paper, about an eighth of a cup of water ran out.

"I've been pumping diesel since I was ten years old. I never knew the garbage that was coming out."

"It's hard to find clean diesel. The Racor would normally take out most of this trash, then it gets plugged up and the engine stops. Most people only hope that they're getting good diesel."

"OK, I'm going to get a filter."

"Just don't let the old man catch you" I said. "Before we leave, come on board. I'd like to show you something."

When we were both in the saloon, I took the engine cover off the Yanmar and pointed to the fuel polishing system.

"Beautiful, what does it do?" he asked.

The lift pump came to life as I threw the switch.

"The fuel is pulled up from the sump at the front of the tank. It runs through the AlgaeX_to kill growth, then the Racor fine filter and finally it flows to the return at the back of the tank. The pump filters about 100 gallons an hour. So if I leave the pump on for an hour if will filter all the diesel twice."

"Wow, you must have the cleanest diesel in the world."

"This diesel is cleaner than when it came from the refinery. All I have to do is add a stabilizer and it will stay that way."

"We have so many diesel engine problems at the Yacht Club. It's usually the injectors. Nobody ever says that the problems are from dirty diesel."

"Who's going to tell Papa that he's got dirty diesel? Besides, your diesel is better than most diesel in the tropics. It's all dirty. Nobody blames the fuel dock unless their Racor plugs up before they get out of the harbor. That's just the way it is. You can filter your diesel or you can have problems."

"I'm not going to tell the old man but I'm going to tell my friends to filter when they fill up."

"You can tell people to filter their fuel. Don't waste your time. Some of them may even try it a couple of times. Most people are not going to use a deck filter until their engine quits and it costs them a thousand dollars to fix their injectors."

Baja Baby

"You're right" he said throwing us the dock lines. "Have a good trip. Where are you headed?"

"We're off to Isla Caja de Muertos" I said.

"You didn't need thirty five gallons to get to Muertos" he said with a laugh.

The dream of sailing is in the warp and weft of every sail. Our ancestors were seduced by the siren song of the ocean. Stand on any shoreline in the world. Be warned that you can be captured by the ocean's eternal mystery, vastness and majesty. There will always be oceans to cross. There will always be people eager to risk their lives to be part of something more significant than themselves. The modern sailboat is our chance to reach out for discovery and adventure. For every sailboat that lies idle, placidly floating at its mooring, there are hundreds of potential sailors who spend their days hoping for their opportunity to sail to the edge of the world. All those who free their minds to venture out into the ocean take pride in the journey.

The modern cruising boat would have been inconceivable to distant generations. In days gone by, explorers eagerly left their homes in search of the dream that lay over the horizon. Today the cruising sailboat is an absolute wonder of modern convenience. GPS is accurate to six inches. Weather fax delivers up to the minute reports. Refrigerators, accurate instruments and the auxiliary diesel engine make the task of exploration a relatively comfortable exercise. What would the sailor of two hundred years ago make of these conveniences? Ironically, as the level of safety and convenience increases in small craft each year, the number of cruisers declines. For every person smitten with the notion of sailing their dreams, only a tiny number put their plans into action. For all of those who are lucky enough to act on their dreams, there is an alarming percentage of first timers that turn around without a fight.

Wendy and I have seen many of the hopeful set sail only to have their hopes of freedom and adventure quashed by an unexpected reality. Storms and dangerous conditions are very low on the list of reasons that sailors lose their momentum. What so often turns people back to port with wrecked hopes of glory is their inflexibility. If the imaginative and the creative are the first people to sign on for adventure, they are also the first to discover the restraints of a life on the waves. It is not the weak or the frightened who give up the cruising life. It is those that can't keep their ice cream hard.

The dream of cruising is nourished by the imagination but it can only be sustained by hopefulness. Any long-term cruiser can spot a person or couple who are about to give up and move on. It begins with the first vague references that things aren't quite right in paradise. A customs agent was surly with them or they were overcharged for a mango. These little complaints mount until the cruisers are lost in their own small world. Perspective becomes introspection. Reality has managed to supersede the dream. The party is over. Buy a horse ranch in Montana.

Baja Baby

If your cruising plans include an auxiliary engine, keep your diesel clean. But most important, be flexible in your expectations and eager to see the world for what it is.

With the dinghy raised in the davits, I unfurled the sails and we set out on a eight mile southeast course for the small island of Isla Caja de Muertos. The name of the island roughly translates to Dead Man's Chest or Coffin Island. From a few miles away, the origin of the name becomes obvious. The island looks like a man laying on his back with his arms crossed on his chest. The island is under the protection of the Government of Puerto Rico ostensibly to protect the indigenous turtle population and to give Puertan Ricans a pleasant place to hang out on the weekend.

The purveyors of folklore are not completely happy with Isla Caja de Muertos characterization as a dead man laying on his back. Another possible explanation for the name of the island dates back to the 1800's when a former merchant sailor named Almeida fell in love with a Basque lady on the island of Curaçao off the coast of South America. Almeida carried his love to St. Thomas in the US Virgin Islands. Shortly after their marriage, the couple pondered Almeida's career choices as a merchant seaman. They both decided that the practical advantages of pirating in the Virgin Islands would offer better prospects for advancement and profit. He and his lovely wife set out aboard his newly requisitioned ship for a bit of pirating mayhem around the Caribbean. Although his wife was a very willing participant in Almeida's new enterprise, she proved inadequate in stopping bullets. On their first raid, she was killed by a musket ball. It was a nasty way to lose your bride. At least he won the conflict.

Almeida had his wife embalmed and placed in a glass box inside a copper coffin. Legend has it that he buried the coffin in a cave somewhere on Caja de Muertos. Just because he was a murdering pirate did not mean that he didn't have a softer side. Apparently he was overcome by uncontrollable grief over his wife's death. Each month he would return to the island to gaze upon her preserved body and leave half of his plundered treasure in her grave. In time, his fast lifestyle caught up with him. Almeida was caught on the Puerto Rican mainland, tried and executed in El Morro in 1832. Many years later, the glass and copper coffin was discovered by a Spanish engineer on Isla Caja de Muertos. Whether the treasure was ever recovered from the coffin remains a secret.

With the tanks full, we motored out of the Bahia de Ponce into a very lively cross chop and raging trade wind.

"Just hold on for a couple more hours and we'll be in a very calm anchorage" I said watching Wendy hold on to a stanchion with white knuckles.

"Hey. I've got an idea that might smooth these troubled waters" she said getting up and disappearing through the companionway. Thirty seconds later she jumped back into the cockpit. "Hit the play button on the CD player" she said with a big smile on her face, concealing a CD cover behind her back.

"OK" I said.

Baja Baby

"And turn it up" she said as I dropped into the saloon and walked to the nav station to start the recording.

The entire boat came to life with the reggae sounds of Bob Marley wailing out the lyrics of his hit tune "Don't worry... about a thing... cause every little thing... gonna be all right." I smiled as I heard her laughter from the cockpit.

"Very good choice" I said sitting beside her.

The wet and wild eight mile jump to Isla Caja de Muertos turned into a two album Bob Marley sail. A good set of waypoints and a strong autopilot brought us right to the anchorage on the southwest corner of the island. We were fortunate that the island blocked practically all of the ocean wave and surge. I dropped the anchor in fifteen feet of beautiful blue Caribbean water on a lightly packed sand bottom.

While I backed down on the anchor and Wendy stowed the main sail, the ferry boat arrived from Ponce with a small handful of local tourists. We listened to their friendly chatter as they disembarked and ran to take one of the covered ramadas near the beach. They had barely arrived before each ramada was overflowing with extended families: mothers, fathers, children and grandparents. Within no time, all of the families were mixing together, sharing food and conversation in an extraordinary display of Puerto Rican civility.

A few hours later, the ferry arrived to carry the party goers back to the mainland. When the ferry captain sounded the boat's whistle right on schedule, ten families looked up in surprise. The mothers scrambled to pack up their chairs, beach towels, coolers, half eaten food and

119

family pets. The fathers and the children made an attempt to pick up the trash that was spread around the tables. The grandfathers finished their cigarettes. In a Puerto Rican minute, they all piled onto the ferry and disappeared into the setting sun. The last sounds of merriment from the boat faded into the distance as the low spine of the island caught the last golden rays of the setting sun. The darkness and silence of the night closed in upon us. The incredible panoramic view of the south shore of Puerto Rico spread out before us. We sat entranced as millions of lights winked on all over the island.

Eleven

Island Time

Our party for two on Isla Caja de Muertos seemed over before it started. Two hours before dawn, we set out on a six hour trip due east. The very protected, mangrove ringed anchorage of Salinas would be our home for the next week. We looked forward to the easy task of having the sail stripe resewn and the more difficult task of replacing the wind transducer and VHF antenna at the mast head.

There are many good anchorages on the south shore of Puerto Rico. The far majority of these isolated anchorages lack even the simplest amenities. Oh my, where's the Coke machine? Cruisers are a diverse group. There exists one great personality contrast in the cruising community. There are party animals and quiet nature seekers. The geriatric party hardy crowd vastly outnumbers the reclusive 'I'd like to be alone now' group.

An all-weather anchorage like Salinas attracts all types. The sociable will jockey to be close to their friends and the restaurants. The not so sociable gravitate to the distant fringes of the anchorage away from the noise, smell and constant dinghy traffic. When we motored into Salinas, I had a number of thoughts on my mind. How was I going to get a hundred pounds plus of sails onto the dock? And where could I find a calm place to climb the mast to remount the electronics? Would the dock of the marina be the right place?

"The docks look crowded. Call the hotel on the handheld and see if they have any space on the dock for one day" I said.

"OK." Wendy keyed the mic. "Marina Salinas, Marina Salinas come in. We would like dockage for one night."

"One moment please" came the reply.

I idled the engine and picked up the binoculars.

"I don't think that they'll charge too much for these docks" I said with a laugh.

The pilings appeared to be driven into the bottom of the bay at odd angles. Each dock board canted at a slightly different angle.

"What do you think Wendy, twenty dollars a night?"

The dock master's voice came over the radio. "We only have one space beside the fuel dock. I can only let you have it for one night."

"Great, one space beside the diesel pumps."

"Do you want to take it?" Wendy asked.

"Ask him what he wants for the slip."

"How much for the night?" Wendy asked.

"Two seventy" he replied.

"Twenty-seven isn't too bad" I said to Wendy.

"David, I think he said two hundred and seventy."

"No way. He must have gotten his Spanglish mixed up. Ask him again."

"Marina Salinas, what did you say the cost for one night was?" Wendy repeated.

"Two hundred and seventy dollars plus tax, electric, water and a disposal fee. That will come to about three hundred."

I took the handheld from Wendy. "Thanks man. I think we'll pass" I said. I turned off the radio. "Well, it looks like we're going to be packing the sails to the dock in the Porta-Potty."

Wendy scanned the anchorage with the binoculars.

"Hey look, someone is picking up right in front of the docks" she said.

I gave the boater a few minutes and motored in to take the spot. We set the anchor in a gooey mud bottom fifty feet from the marina's dock.

"This is going to be a pretty noisy spot. At least we'll only have to be here one night" Wendy said.

"And the best part?" I said.

"What's the best part?" she asked.

"The best part is we won't have to spend three hundred bucks to get aggravated. We can do it for free."

After lunch we busied ourselves with removing and folding the sails as neatly as we could on the deck. Both sails were about twenty-five years old and were cut from nine ounce heavy sailcloth. On the deck, they were heavy and bulky. It was going to be a struggle just to get them in the dinghy. Then there was the quarter mile schlep to the sail loft.

"I think that we're going to need some help carrying the sails to the loft. Let's go over and talk to them" I said.

We left Quest and rode the fifty feet to the dock.

When alongside the dock, I yelled to the dock master "Can we leave our dinghy here for an hour?"

"Sure" he said.

"How much?"

"Don't worry about it. You're going to eat in the restaurant, right" he said with a wink.

"Right" I replied giving him a salute.

We walked into the hotel lobby for directions to the loft.

"Follow the ten foot deep trench up the middle of the road. It will bring you right to Ginger's shop."

A second woman added "Just follow the stink."

As we left the hotel and stepped into the dusty back streets of Salinas, I said to Wendy "This is the famous ten foot Salinas stink trench so highly touted in the tourist guide."

As advertised, the trench brought us on a circuitous path to a hybrid commercial/residential neighborhood of nondescript warehouses and concrete homes.

The Salinas anchorage attracts many boats for many reasons. With so large a fleet of cruising boats in one place, it isn't surprising that the city would develop a thriving marine repair industry. We soon located the sail loft in a small street a short distance from the hotel.

Island Time

"Hello, hello" said a very shrill, disembodied voice.

I spun around. Then I jumped back when I found myself face to face with a beautiful green and blue cockatoo standing on a perch inches away from me. The sail maker looked up from her sewing. She slid her reading glasses to the top of her head.

"Well, you've met Meeter Greeter. Don't worry, he doesn't bite, unless you're a dog" she said. "He absolutely hates dogs. What can I do for you?"

"I called you from La Parguera a week ago. You ordered some green thread for us?"

"So you're Green Stripe. Where are your sails?" she asked.

"They're still on the boat."

"I can't sew them on your boat, hon" she said with a laugh.

A dog hating cockatoo, now a sassy seamstress. Where were we headed?

"We're going to need some help getting the sails down to your shop" I said.

"No problem, a friend of mine will help. Let me give him a call." She went into her office. "He'll be here in twenty minutes. You can wait here" she said politely.

"By the way, what's going on with this sewer project?" I asked.

"Oh that" she said. "Come and take a look. Have you ever heard the expression 'Island Time'? Well, you're looking at it. Three years ago the city council appropriated funds for a new sewer line in this district. They began collecting taxes the next week. Everyone was thrilled that

125

the old leaking system was going to be improved. A month after I got the first tax bill, a crew came down and ripped a huge trench right up the middle of the street. Then they never came back. The merchants complained to the city council. They came back in another year and laid the sewer pipe and connected it to the buildings. The crews left again and didn't come back to fill in the hole. We complained to City Hall again. That was a year ago. Now the pipes are starting to leak and it stinks. When we call City Hall they say 'mañana' and hang up" she said. "Well you're looking at 'Island Time'."

As she finished her discourse on 'Island Time', the door opened and a tall, slim young man of about thirty walked in.

The cockatoo rocked back and forth on his perch before squawking his greeting "Hello, hello."

The young man bowed to the bird and said "Morning, Reefer."

I looked at Wendy, then at Ginger. "I thought the bird's name is Meeter Greeter."

The young man looked at Ginger searching for an answer.

"Reefer is his nickname. You know, like reef your sails" Ginger said shyly. "This is Pepé. He'll help you get the sails off your boat."

As we piled into the front of Pepé's small two seater truck, he gave the trench a wide berth. "Can you believe this mess?" he said commenting on the subterranean, sanitary debacle. "Three years they've been working on this hole. Now the pipes are leaking. The rest

126

of Salinas calls this area The Big Stink."

I looked at Wendy. "They must be working on Island Time" I said with a smile.

"They're definitely on Island Time" Pepé laughed. "Here we are" he said pulling into the hotel's parking lot. My pirogue is tied to the dock over there."

"I hope they didn't charge you too much to leave your boat at the dock" I said.

He looked at me a bit puzzled. "You didn't try to get dock space, did you?"

"Actually we did."

"Three hundred bucks, right?"

"Something like that" I said.

"It's a big boater weekend. The dock price will drop back to normal in a couple of weeks."

We pushed off the dock and motored the short distance to Quest's starboard side.

"That's some heavy sail cloth" Pepé said as we manhandled the dead weight over the toe rail and into the pirogue. "Are you two big ocean cruisers?" he asked.

"No way, Pepé. We're about as green as you'll ever see" I said laughing.

When we arrived back at the sail loft, a wheelbarrow was waiting conveniently at the door. One by one we carried the bulky sails into the loft and dropped them on the table.

Ginger unfolded the yankee and felt the material. "How old are these sails?"

"They're probably a little over twenty-five years old" I replied.

She squeezed the cloth in her right hand. "They look almost brand new."

"We had them re-resined by a company in Pennsylvania."

"What's re-resining? How does it work?"

"The salesman told me that first they give the sails a thorough cleaning, then place them in a bath of resin and fungicide. They're dried in a roller press, then cured by UV light" I said.

"Fancy resin treatment. They don't show much wear, not much at all. Twenty -five years old? Your boat spent most of its life tied to a dock."

"How long will it take to re-sew the stripes?"

"A couple of days" she said.

"Great, we'll give you a call" I said walking towards the door.

When I walked past the cockatoo, it jumped onto my shoulder and began bobbing and weaving. I didn't move as Ginger ran over alarmed. Was the bird an ear biter?

"Reefer, stop that" she yelled.

She enticed the bird with a biscuit. Whenever she got close, the bird jumped to the other shoulder.

"I've never seen him act like this." After a bit more persuading, she managed to get the cockatoo back on the perch. "What are you? Some sort of bird whisperer?" she asked.

"No, he's a big, bad shouter" Wendy said as I opened the door and we walked out into the warm tropical sun. Wendy popped her head back into the shop. "Ginger, where's the closest internet?"

"I don't know about closest, but there's free internet at the library. Hey, Pepé if you're going to town, why don't you give them a lift?"

"Sure, come on" he said "I'll give you a ride."

Pepé graciously dropped us in front of the library a few miles away from the loft.

"Thanks" I said handing Pepé a couple of dollars.

"No need to pay me. Glad to help. Go in that door on the side of the library" he said as he screeched to a halt.

Wendy and I entered the library and walked up to the main desk.

"We'd like to use the internet" I said to the librarian.

"Nine o'clock, nine o'clock."

Wendy looked at the clock on the library wall. "She's cutting it a bit close. It's two minutes to nine."

I stood up from my seat about ten minutes after nine and asked the señora for a PC.

"Nine o'clock" she said with a scowl.

"What time is it?"

"Eight o'clock" she said, pointing to the wall.

"The clock says nine."

"Clock's wrong."

I returned and sat beside Wendy. "She thinks it's eight o'clock. Go talk to her, will you?"

"Sure." Wendy came back with a smile on her face. "Well she's right. Puerto Rico doesn't follow daylight savings time. Nobody does around here."

"Why don't they change the time on the clock?"

"Why do you think? Either they don't know how, they don't care or they're too lazy."

"That's Island Time" we both said in unison.

We went outside and sat in the shade for another hour. At the new nine o'clock, we went back inside. The librarian looked at me like she'd never seen me before.

"Can I help you?" she asked with a blank look in her eyes.

"Can we use the internet?"

"I haven't turned it on. Come back in twenty minutes."

We sat down and waited. Twenty minutes later I asked to use the internet for the third time.

"It hasn't come on yet."

I threw up my hands and stomped out the main door.

When we were outside, I said to Wendy "This is ridiculous. We waited two hours and they still can't get the internet to work."

Right then a man in a suit and tie walked past. Overhearing our conversation, he said "If you have to use the internet, I wouldn't recommend the library. They installed a new system two weeks ago."

"What's the problem?"

"The system isn't the problem. The head librarian is a bit old school. She doesn't think much of computers. She's been the head of the library for fifteen years. If she doesn't want to turn on the computers, they won't come on. Come with me. I run the local government employment bureau next door. We have PCs you might be able to use." He opened the door. "This is ASIFAL. We help people find jobs."

Island Time

The interior was brand new and looked very prosperous. "We don't usually let people come in to use the computers unless they're looking for a job. I'm the Director. I think that I can make an exception this one time" he said.

"We're very grateful" I replied.

"There is just one small problem that I will have to explain before we enter" he said pausing to choose the correct words.

"What's the problem?" Wendy asked.

"It's your attire" he said shyly. You probably don't know this" he paused. "You shouldn't wear shorts or sleeveless shirts in any government building in Puerto Rico. I don't know if it is actually a law. It's just the way it is. Wait here and I will explain the situation to my secretary."

He returned several minutes later. "There are no clients in the office right now. It won't be a problem. If anybody comes in, I may have to ask you to leave."

We walked into the office and the secretary looked in horror at Wendy and me in our sleeveless shirts and shorts.

"No, no" she said rounding her desk. "You can't come in here."

The Director waved his hand in the air. "Marta, they are my guests."

He showed us into his office. "You can use my computer. Just let me take my papers. I'll work in the conference room next door. Come and get me when you're done."

131

A few minutes after the director left, his secretary popped her head into the office. "Would you like coffee or perhaps a beverage?"

"Maybe a glass of water" Wendy said quietly.

She returned a moment later with a serving tray on which sat two bottles of water and six cookies.

"Thank you very much. That was very kind of you" I said.

The secretary placed the tray on the desk and left. I invited Wendy to sit in the director's high back leather chair. I pulled up a stool to the PC.

"Can you believe this? A director of a government office in Puerto Rico invites us in to use his office computers and offers us milk and cookies? How often does that happen?"

"I have no idea" Wendy said.

"Just don't forget to wipe the sweat off his chair when you get up."

Twelve

Work Detail

It was daybreak. We unboxed the brand new wind transducer and radio antenna. Today wouldn't be just a climb. I would be working several hours at the top of the mast. I had a fair guess as to the damage caused by the frigate bird. It was yet to be discovered that the antenna manufacturer had made a small alteration to the antenna base. The new antenna housing would not fit the old base. Some impromptu engineering would be necessary.

Climbing a mast in any conditions is an evocative experience. If you have any degree of vertigo, it will be absolutely soul searching. On a number of occasions, I have seen men climb a 65 foot mast unaided and without mast steps or safety equipment. Not even in my dreams could I imagine shimmying up Quest's slippery aluminum mast like Spiderman.

When climbing was necessary, I went straight by the book. The first piece of equipment that was pulled from the lazarette was the heavy leather safety harness that I had purchased from an arborist supply store in Charlotte, NC.

Quest for the Virgins

The safety harness was cinched around my waist with a stout, one and a half inch leather strap. A stainless steel ring protruded from each side of the harness at my hips. A spare halyard was tied to the harness ring. As I climbed the mast, Wendy would stay on the deck and take the slack out of the line. When at the top of the mast and ready to begin the repairs, the safety halyard would be cleated. With mast steps, safety harness and halyard, it was perfectly safe but also frightening. It would be a good day for a climb.

Safety at the top of the mast can be ensured. It is virtually impossible to fall if the climber is careful. However, the possibility of injury occurring on the deck goes up geometrically with the number of tools and gadgets the person takes up the mast. If a screw driver is accidentally dropped fifty feet, it will hit the deck at about forty miles per hour. A screwdriver traveling at that speed will chip the deck or it might go through your forehead. A fifteen pound cordless power drill would also be traveling at about forty miles per hour. Damage to a deck, port light or person would be considerable from any object falling fifty feet.

Prudence demands a simple course of action for the deck hand that is helping. Don't linger directly underneath someone at the mast head. Tools carried to the mast head must be secured by tether to belt or lanyard. Even sunglasses are tied and secured around the neck.

Waiting for sunrise, I tethered the tools I thought I would need: a slot head and Phillips screw driver, needle nose pliers and a folding knife. Any more than that on the first run would be likely to fall. The rest of the tools sat in a zipped leather bag at the base of the mast. If extra tools were required, Wendy could raise them on another halyard. The only remaining piece of gear was a short length of three strand nylon. This line would be tied to the two rings on the safety harness, then around the mast to allow me to lean back hands-free fifty feet above the deck.

The weather and time of day greatly influence the productivity of someone working at the mast. If the hands are too cold and numb, there is a tendency to drop tools and be clumsy. If the weather is too warm, the hands may sweat to the point that it is hard to turn a screw driver. A mast snapping back and forth at sea is an experience that I wouldn't wish on anyone.

The first brilliant rays of the sun were arching over the mountains of interior Puerto Rico when I began my first ascent of the mast. I slowly opened and locked each step as I progressed. Reaching the top, I asked Wendy to cleat the halyard that was secured to the harness. I removed the short piece of three strand line and connected it to the right side of the harness. I passed it around the mast and tied it to the left side of the harness. After triple checking the knots, I cautiously leaned back and put my weight on the line. I closed my eyes, let go of the mast and let my hands fall to my sides. The blinding fear subsided in seconds. I was feeling light as a feather. I was in the right space.

It was an unusual feeling to be at the masthead looking down at the jumble of boats in the Salinas anchorage. I felt like 'Reefer' on his perch. Time was suspended on wispy, warm updrafts. It was also a good time not to be too casual in a dangerous place.

Salinas ©2015 DigitalGlobe Map Data ©2015 Google

"Send up the tool bag" I called down to Wendy.

She raised the tool bag until it was at my waist. The wind transducer would be a simple replacement. Removing the plastic bag that I had installed over the mast head in Boquerón, I wiped the wind transducer base with a clean rag. After applying a glob of silicone to both the base and the transducer, I screwed the transducer arm into the socket. The operation was over in minutes. The radio antenna was next. I removed the new antenna from the tool bag and tethered it to my harness.

Work Detail

"We have a problem" I shouted down to Wendy. "The electrical connection is the same but it looks like the manufacturer has changed the style of the base."

I descended the mast with the radio antenna in my back pocket.

"There's no way that I can make the old mount fit" I said as I started up the mast to take another look. "The screw heads are completely seized. I'll have to grind them off, then go up again to drill and tap the new holes."

Another trip up the mast with a file and the screw heads were removed. Up the mast for the fourth time with the drill and the correct tap, I was glad to be full of adrenaline. Making four passes to the mast head was the equivalent of climbing 200 feet straight up. With the electronics installed properly, secure and protected from the elements, I waved to Wendy to lower the tool bag and uncleat my halyard. Down I went, one careful step at a time.

At the base of the mast, I said to Wendy "That was a lot more work than I expected. I'm glad I'm done."

We both looked up to the mast head and noticed that I hadn't folded the steps against the mast.

"One more trip" I said with resignation.

"It's my turn now" Wendy said with excitement. She turned and started to climb the mast.

"Get down here" I said.

"Why? I know how to climb the mast" she protested.

"Climb the mast. Have a ball. You just aren't going up there without this" I said handing her the safety harness.

With the harness on and secured to the halyard, Wendy climbed to the top of the mast like a monkey.

"Look" she said holding on with one hand, smiling and waving. "I should have brought the camera. It's a great view up here."

As Wendy descended and folded the mast steps, the owner of a neighboring boat came out on deck.

"I'm heading to Culebra. Want to sail over with me?" he said turning on his engine.

"No" I said. "I have to test the electronics."

"Maybe I'll see you there."

He started his windlass and began to pull in his anchor rode as Wendy stepped back on the deck.

"Boy this rode seems light today" he said.

Wendy and I cringed as the end of the rode came out of the water without the anchor attached.

"Man, can you believe it? The anchor came loose" he yelled in frustration.

"Don't worry about your anchor right now. We can get it later. Motor over beside Quest and we'll tie you off."

We caught his lines and held his boat secure.

"I don't know what happened. I just bought the anchor two days ago."

"I haven't heard of seizing wire breaking that soon. It must have had some sort of flaw" I said.

"Seizing wire, what's that?"

I glanced at Wendy in disbelief. "The eye in the shackle? Did you run a piece of wire through the hole in the shackle screw?"

"Oh the hole. I saw the hole. I thought it was a hole

for a screw driver. You know, to tighten the shackle. What am I going to do? It's my only anchor."

"We'll find your anchor. First we have to mark the spot where you think it is. Come on, lets get into the dinghy."

Tying a fender at the end of a length of line, we pushed off.

"Where do you think you dropped the anchor?" I asked.

"Just over there" he said.

We paddled over. After tying the dinghy anchor to the fender line, I dropped it into the water.

"At least we can tell where your anchor is now. That's the first step" I said. "By the way, what's your name?" I asked.

"Jeremy" he answered.

"Well, glad to meet you. What do you think we should do now?" I said.

"The only thing I can do is dive in and look around for the anchor."

"The anchor's not going anywhere. Let's go back on Quest and think about it" I said.

As I climbed aboard Quest, I noticed Jeremy's hands shaking as he went up the swim ladder.

"Sit down and have a glass of water" I said.

"No thanks, I have to get in the water and find my anchor."

I motioned Wendy to get a glass of water.

When he took the water, I spoke to him quietly. "You might want to consider a couple of things before you just dive in and start mucking about."

"It's my only anchor. It's brand new. I can't afford another anchor."

"New anchor or not, I'm going to tell you why you shouldn't dive in there."

"OK" he said looking down.

"Look around you. There's a hundred boats pumping waste into the anchorage. The city dumps ten times that amount in twenty minutes. This isn't water. It's a biological weapons lab. Dive in there unprotected and you'll be taking some very serious chances. You may even live to regret it."

"I never really thought about it."

"The water is just the start. The really bad stuff is at the bottom in the muck. This little harbor never gets flushed. There's human bacteria down there from 1000 B.C. Here's an idea" I said opening the lazarette. "I'll set up the hookah and teach you how to use it. The goggles will protect your eyes. If you can remember to keep your mouth shut, you should be OK."

"Sounds good. Let's get going" he said.

I pulled the hookah and the air hose out of the locker.

"Wendy, could you get the weights and mask?"

As Wendy went into the cabin for the diving gear, a dinghy pulled alongside Quest.

"Hey, what's going on Jeremy?"

Jeremy smiled and said "This is David and Wendy. They're helping me find my anchor. It came loose from the rode this morning."

Work Detail

"I'm Marianne" the woman said. "What have you got there?" she said.

"That's his hookah. I'm going to dive for the anchor as soon as he shows me how to use it."

Marianne looked at me. "What do you need all that for? The water's only fifteen feet deep. What a bunch of wimps. The anchor is below that fender?"

Before I had a chance to say yes, Marianne was over the side of the dinghy. The water was so opaque that we lost sight of her when she was only a few inches underwater. A minute later she bobbed to the surface and spit out a mouthful of brown water and coughed.

"I found it. I got my finger on it. I'm going back down and tie the end of the float line to it. Then you can pull it up. OK?" she said self-assured.

Down she went. On surfacing again, she spit out another mouthful. She was covered from head to waist in brown sludge.

"Take this" she said handing me the dinghy line.

I looked at Wendy then at Jeremy. "It might be a good idea to pull up the anchor on your foredeck" I said handing him the line.

Wendy, Jeremy, and I jumped across to his boat. We had no problem lifting the anchor onto the deck.

"What about me?" Marianne said beginning to climb Quest's swim ladder.

I looked at her and shuddered. I could barely recognize a human being underneath the brown slime.

"Hold on there. Why don't you climb into your dinghy instead" I suggested politely.

141

She gave me a withering brown frown and rolled lithely over the gunnels of her dinghy.

"My work is done. I'm outta here. Great plan you guys had. It's a good thing I showed up" she said pulling the start cord of her dinghy engine.

Jeremy cupped his hands over his mouth. "Hey Marianne, can I buy you lunch?"

"Nope, some other time" she said streaking towards the hotel dinghy dock.

When she pulled up to the dock and started to get out of the dinghy, the dock master ran out of his shack and screamed "No. No, stop!"

The rest of the conversation between the dock master and 'Mud Girl of the Lagoon' was largely inaudible except for the loud and punctuated string of profanity coming from Marianne. Ignoring the protests of the dock master, she jumped on the dock, grabbed the garden hose and proceeded to wash down.

Jeremy reattached the anchor to the end of his rode and tightened the shackle. I handed him a foot of Monel seizing wire that I had cut from the spool.

"So that's seizing wire" he said.

"Run it through the hole in the shackle, then around the shackle loop and make a few twists."

Jeremy looked up as he threaded the seizing wire. "Can you believe Marianne? What an Amazon. She didn't need diving gear" he said with a wistful expression on his face.

I looked at Wendy and smiled. "Yeah, she's quite the woman when she's hosed down."

Work Detail

When the anchor was safely stowed, I threw Jeremy his dock lines and he motored away.

"Still going to Culebra?" Wendy asked.

"No, I think I'll stick around and see if I can find Marianne" he said with a smile.

After giving our hands a thorough wipe with alcohol, I turned on the instruments. It was fantastic to watch the wind direction come up on the screen.

"It looks like the new wind transducer is working fine" Wendy said.

"With a bit of calibration, it might even give us the right direction" I said. "Let's try the new radio antenna."

Wendy turned on the VHF. "No sparks, no shocks. That's a good sign."

"Here goes" I said. "Hello, hello, this is a radio check to all stations. Come in."

I got no response.

"Uh oh" Wendy whispered.

"Give them a chance to answer" I said.

"Quest, this is Brigadoon. You're coming in 'five by five', Mr. Holloran!"

"What is that supposed to mean?" Wendy asked.

"Blackboard Jungle?"

Wendy shrugged.

"He's telling me we're coming in loud and clear. I think we can safely say that the radio is working fine."

"Where are you Brigadoon?"

"I'm between Puerto Rico and Vieques. Where are you?" he asked.

"We're in Salinas."

"Wait a minute, I'll look on the chart" he said fading in and out. "This is Brigadoon back at you. It looks like your radio can reach at least thirty miles."

"That should work. If you're in Salinas tomorrow, I'll buy you a beer. Over and out."

"This is Ginger at the loft. I heard your radio check. You're coming in great. Who is Mr. Holloran?"

"Forget about it. How are the sails coming?"

"I have them almost done. You can pick them up tomorrow. Come early."

"Great" I said.

"I hear that you had some excitement this morning" she said.

"I guess so. I climbed the mast."

"Not that. I heard someone lost their anchor. A girl came through the shop about a half hour ago bragging about diving on someone's anchor and saving the day. Is that true? Did she really dive in the bay without a mask? Why didn't you stop her?"

"Stop her? Some people you don't want to stop" I said.

"I hear you, over."

Thirteen

Get Up and Go

The last chore in Salinas was to pick up and install the two repaired headsails.

"Boy, this dock is getting busy. What's going on?" Wendy said as we dinghied in.

When the dock master caught the painter he asked "How long you gonna be?"

Had we outstayed our welcome that soon?

"Not too long. We're just going down the road to pick up something" I said.

"Be back by noon. This place is going to get pretty crazy."

"No problem. Expecting a crowd?"

He looked at me blankly. "Easter?" he said inquisitively.

"What about Easter?"

"Tomorrow's Easter."

"Well, happy Easter."

"You don't know, do you?" he said.

"Sure I know about Easter."

"I don't think you really know."

Here we go. I braced for his rousing perspective on the joy of salvation. I looked at Wendy. She fidgeted in the dinghy doing her best to stay as far from the discussion as possible.

"Come up on the dock" I said to Wendy. "He's going to tell us about Easter."

I watched Wendy try to disappear. The dock master raised his hands over his head.

Reaching into the firmament, he began his sermon. "Easter." He paused for effect. "Easter is about the biggest boat holiday we have in Puerto Rico. Within three hours, this dock is gonna be Party Central. If you're planning to sleep tonight, I'd anchor way out there" he said pointing about a quarter mile up into the mangroves.

"It gets that bad? I thought that Puerto Ricans were pretty religious" I said teasing.

"Hey, Lent's over. You're about to see our other side" he said with a boisterous laugh. "One more thing" he said as Wendy and I walked to the end of the dock. "The police boat and marine patrol will be here soon."

"For the celebration?"

"No, not to celebrate. They're here to write this year's quota of speeding tickets to all the Puerto Ricans."

"Just Puerto Ricans?"

He looked at Quest and laughed. "A sailboat? You're safe. I doubt if you're going to break the speed limit anywhere."

"We'll be back as soon as possible. We're picking up our sails at the loft."

"No problem. Say hi to Reefer."

"Let's get the lobby to call a cab" I said to Wendy as we walked through the parking lot.

"He knows Reefer" Wendy laughed.

"Reefer? Yeah. Puerto Rico is full of natural resources. There's the El Yunque rain forest in the north and Reefer the toking cockatoo on the south shore" I said as we stepped into the air conditioned lobby. "Can you call us a cab?" I asked the receptionist.

"I don't need to call you a cab" she said. "Every cab in town is going to show up here twice today. Wait over by the door, you'll see."

"How much would a cab be for about half a mile?"

"Not much." She paused. "Picking something up?" she asked.

"A couple of sails" I said.

She whistled between her teeth. "Don't tell the cabby about the two sails until they're in the trunk. And get in quick. Better yet, let me see if I can round up Rondo. I see his truck in the parking lot." She picked up a walkie talkie. "Rondo, qué pasa" she said.

"Nada Baby."

"¿Puede darle a alguien un corto paseo?" (Can you give someone a short ride?)

"Sí, mi amor, cualquier cosa por ti nena."

The receptionist blushed as Wendy grinned and laughed. "I don't think you two were supposed to hear that" she said shyly.

Two minutes later, Rondo rolled through the lobby door.

"So you two are the someone" he said smiling seductively at the receptionist. "OK, lets go" he said to us.

As soon as were all squeezed into the two-seater truck, he turned on the radio and started to sing along with a pop tune.

"Everybody seems so happy today" Wendy said to Rondo.

"Sí sí, it's Easter. Lent's over. We celebrate now."

"Isn't today Saturday?" I asked.

"Hey, close enough. It's been a long Lent" he said reaching over and turning up the radio.

Rondo parked in front of the loft and turned off the engine.

"I'll wait here. Put the sails in the back" he said slouching down in the seat and pulling his cap over his eyes.

"How'd you know we were picking up sails?" I asked.

He pointed down to the steering wheel of the truck. "Truck" he said. Then he pointed to the sail loft. "Sail loft. Why would two gringos sit on one seat in this bone shaker unless they wanted to pick up some sails for free?" he said sliding back down into the seat.

"Not so free" I said.

He smiled.

"We'll be right back."

"I'm good. Don't hurry for me" he said.

Get Up and Go

Wendy got off my lap and avoided the sewer trench. She started to open the door of the loft.

"Hold on. Stand back. Let me open it" I said with a grin.

I opened the door and stepped through.

"Hello, Hello" I said to Reefer.

Reefer gave out one long squalk, wings spread, feathers flew, and a second later, the cokatoo landed on my head. Ginger looked up from the sewing machine nonplused as I walked towards her with the cockatoo bobbing and weaving on top of my head.

"Are you two trying out for the circus?" she laughed. "By the way, it's a lot easier to get a cockatoo on your head than off. Come on Reefer" she said holding her hand to my forehead. "Your sails are over by the door" she said relocating Reefer onto the perch. "They came out great" she said beaming.

"I don't want to rush you but we have a truck waiting outside" I said.

"There was a small problem with the job. You know I had to send to Germany for a full spool of thread. The shipping cost more than the thread. I only used about half. Do you want the rest of the spool? I can't use it."

"Sure" Wendy said.

"Also, I don't normally charge for needles but" she paused. "This green thread was so stiff I broke a bunch before I figured out how to use it."

"No big deal" I said.

Wendy took the bill from Ginger and paid in cash.

"Let me help you out to the truck. I'm closing up. It's party time" she said.

"So I've heard."

Opening the door she saw Rondo asleep behind the wheel. She stuck her head through the open passenger window. "¿Rondo, qué pasa?"

Rondo looked up with a frown which quickly turned to a smile. "Ginger baby, hola. Give me a kiss."

"Give your wife a kiss. How about a ride to the marina, Rondo?" she asked.

"Sure" he said.

I jumped onto the narrow passenger seat. "Wait a second, let me slide the seat back" I said.

Wendy sat on my lap and Ginger sat on Wendy's lap. Rondo put the old truck in gear.

He slapped me on the arm and laughed. "Better watch what you hold onto when we take the corners."

There wasn't a parking space to be had as Rondo pulled past the hotel. On the marina dock, the Holy Saturday crowd had increased into a small mob.

"You're never going to get down the dock with those sails" Rondo said. "I'll park over by the break wall."

Ginger and Rondo helped us unload the sails. Then they disappeared into the throng.

"Stay with the sails. I'll get the dinghy" I said to Wendy.

Crossing the parking lot I waded into the dense crowd on the dock. As I pushed through the families, women embraced me and half a dozen men tried to put a can of beer in my hand. I took two. They were only ten

150

ounce. I found the dinghy and jumped down.

"I told you it was going to get crazy" said the dock master passing me the painter. "I'm glad you came back. I've had to stop three people from stealing your dinghy."

"Only three?" I said.

"Maybe only one" he said laughing.

As I pushed off he said "Hold on. You're going to need one of these." He opened a cooler on the dock and threw me a cold one. "Feliz Pascua" he said.

"Felix Pasquale to you too" I said, raising a can of Medalla Light.

Motoring around the corner, I found Wendy sitting on the sail bags at the edge of the break wall under the shade of a mangrove.

"Let's get out of here. This place is getting crazy" I said.

Pushing off from the dock, we were at Quest's stern in minutes. We soon had the sails manhandled onto the deck. I lubricated both head sail luff tubes. We had the sails raised and cleated in record time.

"Go start the engine. I'm pulling up the anchor."

"I was hoping you'd say that."

I swung Quest around and pointed her to the ocean. On the way out of the crowded anchorage, we both noticed the police boat and the marine patrol anchored very conspicuously right in the middle of the channel. Wendy and I waved as we passed. The crews of both the police boat and the marine patrol completely ignored us as we approached.

"Watch this" I said to Wendy as I nudged Quest

within a few feet of the police boat. "Hola, Felix Pasqueso" I said nodding to the officers.

The commanding officer looked at me with a blank look on his face. "¿Qué?"

"Felix Pasqueso" I repeated.

He stared at me. Then the entire crew broke up in fits of snickering as we motored by.

"Keep your speed down" one of the officers laughed. "And a happy Easter cheese to you too" he added.

My original plan was to simply re-anchor at the far end of the bay. The further we motored, the larger the crowd became. Who could blame them? It was a beautiful day to be on the water. Ten or more groups of rafting boats occupied the majority of the little space remaining outside the main channel.

"We can't anchor here. Too many boats. Would you enter the waypoints for Cayos Caribes in the GPS?"

"I'm way ahead of you. I loaded them last night."

We left the Easter crowd behind as we motored from Bahia Salinas. Carefully navigating our way through the shallow waters of the inside passage, we arrived at Cayos Caribes an hour later. Cayos Caribes is a chain of small, low barrier islands a few miles east of the Salinas anchorage which stretch across the mouth of Bahia de Jobos. The islets form a natural ocean break wall for the Bahía de Jobos National Estuarine Research Reserve. Much of the Reserve is far too shallow for deep draft sailboats. The small deep anchorage behind the barrier islands would provide a very tranquil anchorage for the night.

Get Up and Go

There was a striking contrast between the placid calmness of the lagoon and the raging Caribbean crashing against the reef only a few hundred feet away. There was an even greater contrast between Cayos Caribes and Salinas. Salinas is a very popular harbor filled with boats and activity. The cool ocean breeze was very welcome after the sweltering conditions in closed-in Salinas Bay. Cayos Caribes was only a few miles from Salinas but a world apart from the crowds and pollution of the bay.

"What do you say, time for a swim before lunch?" I said.

We both immediately stripped down and, as always, raced each other to be the first over the side. After the obligatory splashing session, we both settled down to back floating. I went to the bow and enmeshed my toes into the links in the anchor chain. The warm, calm water near the beach relaxed me into a cat nap.

"Come look at this" Wendy said.

"What's up?"

"Put your hand under the hull and feel the bottom."

I ran my hand under the water line.

"I see what you mean."

There wasn't any hard barnacle growth, but there was a heavy layer of slime.

"It's always a good time to pull out the hookah and scrub the bottom" I said returning to the cockpit.

Wendy pulled out the mask, fins and snorkel while I warmed up the air compressor.

"I thought you scrubbed the bottom not too long

ago" Wendy said tethering the large scotch-brite brush to my wrist.

"It wasn't that long ago. Trash really seems to build up when we're in the mangroves. Luperon was a lot worse. This is probably just a coating of mangrove mud and sewage" I said descending the stern swim ladder.

As was our routine, Wendy stayed on deck to make sure that the compressor kept running and the hoses didn't tangle.

"I'll see you in a couple of hours" I said putting my mask on.

Cleaning Quest's bottom is a task that I always enjoyed even if I didn't always look forward to it. Below the water line is a different world. Sound is particularly distorted. It took me a minute or two to identify the crashing waves of the Caribbean on the far side of the barrier island. It was a loud, pulsing shushing sound that felt like it carried subsonics. Shush, bang... shush, bang. The mid-tones were constant and eerie, like a strong wind blowing through a pine forest.

Taking my starting position at the rudder with the suction cups in my left hand and the brush in my right, I began the job. As soon as I started to clean the hull, the normal complement of tiny fish arrived from nowhere to feast on the hull scrapings. Within five minutes the predator fish showed up to feed on the small fish. I didn't have to wait long. By the time that I had completed the stern and was half way up the starboard side, I saw the first quick flash of a very long fish. It streaked past my right periphery. Avoid eye contact with barracuda. I closed my eyes and turned my head slowly to avoid alarming the creature. When I peeked through one eye, there wasn't one; there were two small barracuda staring into my mask about a foot away. It's not their bulk that will scare you. It is their evil, primordial slackjaw smile and their needle-sharp teeth. 'Just go about your business and try to ignore them' I thought as I continued to the port side of the hull. Occasionally they would make a lunge for a minnow or piece of floating debris. Just when I thought I had become comfortable with my slackjaw minnow-eaters, they both developed an interest in my diving mask. Turning towards the boat, I finished the rear quarter.

A moment later I heard the improbable sound of laughter. I peeked from side to side. The barracuda were gone. I heard the laughter again. I was sure of it. 'Wendy's probably playing the radio' I thought as I continued cleaning the hull. Then I felt a tug on the air hose. Looking up through the surface of the water, I saw Wendy jumping up and down excitedly. I surfaced immediately.

"Did you see the pod of dolphins? There were five dolphins" she said.

"You mean barracuda?"

"The barracuda split when the dolphins showed up. The dolphins came within a few inches of you. Didn't you hear them?"

"I thought I heard laughter."

"That was the dolphins. It might have been laughter. They sure looked happy enough. They came racing into the anchorage about ten minutes ago. Then the barracuda took off like missiles. At first I thought the dolphins were sharks. They weren't too big. I figured you could handle them."

"Give me ten more minutes and I'll be be finished" I said.

I gave the last part of the stern a good wipe down. It was time to surface. I climbed the swim ladder slowly, adjusting from the buoyancy of the water. I looked down at my chest. Without my glasses, it looked like I was covered in blotchy mud. Wendy came closer with a look of terror in her eyes.

"That isn't dirt. You're covered in bugs" she screamed.

I put on my glasses and recoiled. I was covered from head to toe in tiny, crawling marine creatures no larger than the head of a small button.

"Get back in the water and clean off. They're crawling everywhere" Wendy said pushing me down the ladder.

I landed in the water with a thump and a splash.

"This is really creepy. Use the scrub brush. Take your shorts off and shake them."

I scrubbed and shook for ten minutes. The small bugs were everywhere. They were in my hair, the pockets of my shorts, my ears.

"I'm coming back on board."

"You better have all the bugs off."

"I've got most of them."

"Forget most, get all of them."

After a thorough inspection, I stepped back in the cockpit and asked Wendy for my glasses.

Get Up and Go

"Bring up one of the microscopes. Take a look at this" I said. "They look like perfectly formed baby crabs."

"I don't care what they look like. Get them out of here."

I later identified the tiny creatures as hermit crabs in the megalopae cycle. It was a good year for crabs and cruisers in the Jobos National Reserve.

Fourteen

Trading Winds

For two months we plunged headlong into the trade winds. The pleasant memories of the Dominican Republic would stay with us forever. The anchorages and places that we had visited were nothing less than spectacular. It was the constant and relentless close hauling in heavy seas that lost its luster. Sailing in practically any condition is an occupation that will set you free. Two months of constant tacking, shrieking wind and wet plunges into head seas was a rite of passage that was accepted. The thorny path is a rigorous trial. It is not a pleasure cruise. When we began our fight into the trade winds, we were filled with the hope that the horrors of the thorny path were an exaggeration. In the end we were luckier than some. Quest and crew survived. We closed the book on the thorny path when we passed through the small opening in the reef at Cayos Caribes to continue our journey.

We were conditioned to heavy sailing. The sea was predicted to be a very modest three feet. The accompanying wind was mild and offshore. When the depth gauge read thirty feet, I walked nonchalantly to the mast and raised the main as comfortably as a Sunday sailor. The ocean was surprisingly calm. Even the distant horizon seemed as smooth as a ruler. Returning to the cockpit I studied the weather fax.

"Just when you thought we would be fighting the trades for the rest of our lives, the wind changes" I said to Wendy.

"I don't care if it's just a one day reprieve. I'm ready for a comfortable sail" she replied.

When the twenty mile course for Puerto Patillas was entered into the GPS, both head sails were unfurled. We were off for a beautiful six hour trip along the rugged south coast of Puerto Rico.

Many of the larger islands in the Caribbean have dramatic variations in precipitation. The annual precipitation in Puerto Rico's El Yunque national rain forest in the northeast exceeds 200 inches. That is seventeen feet of rainfall per year. When it doesn't rain for two days in El Yunque, it makes the news. This enormous amount of precipitation is the factor that keeps one of the world's biological engines running. In comparison, the arid south coast of Puerto Rico receives about 35 inches on average. Our twenty mile sail de jour from Cayos Caribes to Puerto Patillas would give us a sailor's view of south Puerto Rico's incredible contrast in rainfall and terrain.

On the west three quarters of the south coast of Puerto Rico, flat plains extend inland to meet the rugged central mountain chain. These fertile lowlands support much of Puerto Rico's agriculture. In terms of sheer volume, sugar cane dominates all other crops. This easily grown grass is well suited to the soil and climate. It has limited use as a food crop. But it does fuel a thriving rum industry on an island where every job counts. Dwarfed by sugar but still important agriculturally are the production of rice, mangoes, avocados, maize, and coffee. Agriculture is a dicey business anywhere. In Puerto Rico, a farmer's life can be turned upside down in a heartbeat. Hurricanes frequently destroy crops that are days from harvesting. As I looked out onto the bucolic scene of thousands of acres of cane, I was struck with the irony that when the next Category 5 hurricane blows all the sugar cane into the Caribbean, the Bacardi rum distillery in San Juan won't skip a beat. There is always plenty of sugar cane grown somewhere and there is always plenty of Bacardi rum on the world's shelves.

Sailing closer to Puerto Patillas, the massive mountains of the interior seemed to force their way right down to the shoreline. The row crops of sugar cane and maize disappeared to be replaced with the more natural looking mango and avocado trees that are more suited to the hill country.

As we made our approach to the Puerto Patillas anchorage, the geometrically perfect fields of the western flatland gave way to hill country. Tropical, lush, dark green vegetation thrived on rolling hills that cascaded to the shoreline.

We entered the very wide open bay and found the

anchorage behind a very substantial reef. It would give us all the protection we needed from the sea. When the anchor was dropped and set in a sandy gravel bottom, I returned to the cockpit before securing the mainsail.

"That was about the best sail I think we've ever had. I was starting to forget how much fun it can be" I said.

"I agree. Two months of fighting for every inch... this feels like cheating" Wendy said.

"By the look of this weather fax, the wind will be favorable for at least another five days. There aren't any storms within five hundred miles. If the conditions don't change we have some great sailing ahead. Maybe the worst is behind us" I replied.

It really is fantastic to be in a beautiful, calm anchorage. It was absolutely wonderful to have a six hour sail unmarred by the physically depleting effects of fighting a raging ocean that seemed bent on our destruction. We didn't know it quite yet, nor would we have believed it, but Puerto Patillas marked the finish line of the Thorny Path.

Filled with guarded optimism and bonne vie, I turned to Wendy and asked "If you could eat any meal I can make, what would it be?"

"Spaghetti and meat balls" was her immediately reply.

"You've got to be kidding" I said.

"Nope, that's what I want today."

"OK, that's what it's going to be. Let's have that last bottle of good Chianti we bought in the DR."

"Perfect" Wendy said.

With the waning orange light of sunset reaching far into the cabin, I soaked and drained a half cup of TVP and mixed it with mashed chick peas, bread crumbs, onion powder, garlic, dried basil, oregano, red pepper flakes, a sprinkle of Kikkoman and a pinch of ground fennel. When the mixture was doughlike, I turned it over to Wendy to roll into small half inch 'meatballs'.

"We have some bottled marinara that I might be able to work on" I said.

"Improve away" she said.

Chopping a quarter of an onion very finely, I dropped it in a buttered pan with a clove of garlic and a few herbs. When it was translucent, I deglazed the pan with a few tablespoons of Chianti and added half a bottle of marinara. While the sauce simmered on the right burner, I fried up the 'meat balls' until they were light brown, then added them to the sauce to absorb moisture.

"Hey, we still have half a stick of french bread. It isn't green yet" Wendy said as she pulled the chilled Chianti from the refrigerator.

"Bring it out. It's a bit dry. I'll see if I can revive it."

A light sprinkle of sea water and it was placed directly in the oven on a low heat for a few minutes.

"Sea water on the bread. Nice touch" Wendy said.

"We'll see. I never tried it before."

After boiling the angel hair for about three minutes, I mixed it with the sauce and meatballs. Moments later we were sitting at the cockpit table with a good meal before us.

"You know Wendy, when you first said spaghetti and meat balls, it didn't immediately grab me. When you look out over this landscape we could be off the coast of Genoa, Italy."

"It does look like the Mediterranean. Buona pasta " she said smiling and raising her glass.

A few hours after sunset, cool air began to slide down the side of the mountains and bring a chill into the cockpit.

"I'm going to get a sweater. Can I get you something?" Wendy asked.

"Nah. Let's just clean up the dishes and go to bed" I said.

Gathering the dishes we descended into the warmth of the cabin and closed the companionway door.

"Let's get up early and walk to Patillas" I said.

"Walk to Patillas? I don't think so. It's nine miles. Let's get a ride" she said.

"Happy Easter" I said turning off the light.

"And a Felix Pasqueso to you too" she said with a chuckle.

Puerto Patillas stood out as one of the south shore's great enigmas. It is an easy anchorage to navigate and the holding is perfect, yet it is rarely used by cruisers. The next day as we ate breakfast we counted no less than seven sailboats offshore. In the afternoon another flotilla sailed by in loose formation. No one stopped. Cruisers sail in groups and will vie for the last thirty feet of space in a crowded anchorage. Conversely they will avoid an empty anchorage like the black plague.

We lowered the dinghy and set off for our adventure to Patillas. Before the night dew was dry on the vegetation, we hit the shore line.

"Should we lock the dinghy to a tree?" Wendy said as we pulled the boat high up on the beach.

"Nobody's going to steal a Porta-Potty. It's safe."

Climbing the slight incline of the beach brought us to a narrow dusty trail. The flamboyant trees that grew a few hundred feet inland were in full bloom and sported a magnificent canopy of brilliant red orange flowers tipped with golden highlights.

A short walk through a cool tropical forest brought us to a hardtop secondary road.

"Patillas is probably that way" I said turning left into the bright sunlight where the heat of the morning was beginning to penetrate.

We began walking up the center of the road which would eventually lead us to the main highway to Patillas where we might get a ride into town.

"I think I hear a car coming fast. We better get to the side of the road."

As we stepped back to the shoulder, an old rusty truck without a muffler came thundering around the corner. When the driver saw us, he swerved. I only had time to say "jump" before he slammed on the brakes. Wendy and I ended up in a dry, shallow ditch. The driver turned off the noisy engine and slid out of the truck.

"Sorry, sorry, sorry" he exclaimed throwing his hands up in the air. "I'm really sorry. I didn't see you. This piece of junk doesn't have any brakes on the left side. When I brake hard, it pulls to the right. I hope you didn't think I was trying to run you down."

He walked up to me, grabbed my hand and started pumping my arm.

"Where are you going today?" he asked.

"Patillas" I said a little breathless.

"Come on, I'll make sure you get there" he said.

Wendy barely had closed the door before he took off in a cloud of dust and screeching tires.

"Let me guess" he said over the growl of an un-muffled big block Chevy. "I bet you're going to the Super Plaza."

I looked at Wendy. She nodded.

"How'd you know?" I said.

The nine mile trip to Patillas was a blur of twists and turns on a hilly country road.

"Here it is" he said pulling in front of a grocery store. "If they don't have it, you don't need it. I don't know if it's true, but that's what their ad says in the Sunday paper" he said as Wendy shut the truck's door.

Quest was still well provisioned from Salinas. We did more gawking than buying. With a bag of fresh local fruit, vegetables and a case of 10 oz beer we walked back to the side of the road to catch a minibus to the anchorage. We didn't wait more than a minute before the next bus swerved around the corner.

"This one is going in the right direction" I said trying to flag the driver.

He didn't even slow down. He didn't even look at us.

"What's going on?" Wendy said.

Another bus passed us without stopping. Then a

third thundered by blasting his horn.

Walking back to the store, I asked a well-dressed cashier why the buses didn't stop for us.

She smiled and said "They're full. You have to catch them at the bus depot. Mia" she shouted.

A beautiful mulatto teenager came running to the counter.

"Take these people to the bus terminal" she ordered.

"That's OK. Just tell us where it is" I insisted.

"Nonsense, this is Mia. She'll bring you there and make sure you catch the right bus."

Mia shyly took the bag of groceries that Wendy was carrying and walked out the front door.

"You better follow her. She's getting away" the cashier said laughing.

"Mia, Mia slow down" I shouted from the entrance.

We caught up with Mia halfway across the parking lot. She turned around and gave us a gorgeous heart melting smile.

"I'm David and this is Wendy" I said.

"Hello Mr. David" she said continuing her fast pace through the parking lot. "The bus terminal isn't far. Follow me. That was the manager Señora Pérez you talked to in the store. She is very strict."

Mia wasn't a big talker. That was the last word we heard from her until we reached the terminal.

"Sit here" she said pointing to a bench under a shade awning. "You're going to the port, sí?"

"Yes we have a boat in the bay" I said.

Trading Winds

"Then take number 18 to Lamboglia. It goes right past the beach."

I turned around to find the departure time on the board. When I turned back, she was gone.

"We're lucky. The next bus leaves in five minutes" I said.

We boarded the empty Lamboglia bus. The departure time came and went. A few more people climbed on the bus. Another half hour passed.

"Some schedule" I said getting up.

I stepped out of the bus and approached a group of men playing checkers.

"When does the bus leave?"

A bus driver snapped his fingers, frowned at me and said "When it's full."

He returned his full concentration to the game. An hour and a half passed. The last seat was taken by an old man who sat in the seat opposite me.

The driver looked up and yelled "OK" while swiping all the checker pieces off the board and into a small paper sack. "We go" he said with the authority of a General as he closed the door and started the engine.

The bus clanked and groaned down the hills to the bay. When the blue Caribbean was in sight, the old gentleman sitting beside me leaned over and said in almost a whisper "Have you seen the reef?"

"What reef?" I asked.

"That reef" he said pointing to a spit of land at the end of the bay.

"You can walk right out to it from the beach.

STOP" he said tapping the bus driver on the shoulder. "Get out here" he said motioning us to the door.

We walked the short distance into the forest and down to the beach.

"We don't have anything frozen. Why don't we take a look at the reef before we go back to Quest" I said to Wendy.

"Sure" Wendy agreed.

A quarter mile stroll down the beach brought us to a rocky point of land.

"There it is" Wendy said pointing.

"There's what?" I said.

From a distance, the reef looked like a big pile of submerged gray rocks. As we waded into the reef, the coral formations began to take on tremendous definition. Looking straight down, they came to life. Schools of powder blue parrot fish with florescent pink stripes swam among the flashy yellow fire coral. Brilliant purple and yellow staghorn coral grew in the higher spots with the more subtle brown-gray brain coral filling in the bottom. We stood in water up to our waist and watched an amazing display of multi colored angel fish, butterfly fish and schools of small trumpet fish milling about our legs.

"You know, we would have never seen this reef if the old man hadn't pointed it out" I said to Wendy.

"Yeah, you kind of wonder what everybody's missing" Wendy said as we carefully stepped through the coral on our way back to the beach.

Fifteen

Green Beach Invasion

We were lulled to sleep at night by a gentle, rolling ocean surge that lapped lazily over the reef. We awoke very early to the purple light of false dawn. As the sky brightened, we readied ourselves and Quest for another beautiful sail.

"The gods are smiling on us again" I said removing the sail cover.

The weather system that had brought picture perfect conditions while we were in Cayos Caribes would hold strong for at least another week. With the warm morning sun in our faces, we made a wide sweep around the reef's eastern tip that jutted into the Caribbean. Clearing the headland, I raised the main and unfurled all the sails our little boat carried.

"This is going to be easy" I said. "It's over there" I said pointing confidently to the island of Vieques, a small dot on the horizon.

"We won't need the GPS today" Wendy said as she engaged the autopilot.

Quest settled into a fast starboard tack. Stepping down into the galley, I pulled the pin of the gimbal break on the stove. Quest was heeling at about thirty degrees. The seas were flat with practically no roll. It would be a good day to cook the other 'Breakfast of Champions'. I tightened a sauce pan into the fiddles, added two cups of water and a pinch of salt.

"Couscous in ten minutes" I said to Wendy in the cockpit.

"Couscous. Don't you just love saying couscous?" Wendy yelled over the wind.

"It sure sounds more romantic than crushed semolina" I said with a laugh.

When it was cooked, I added a handful of raisins, cashews and a tablespoon of butter. After stirring in the good stuff, I left the pot on the burner to steam for five minutes.

Green Beach Invasion

"Here you go" I said handing Wendy two bowls of warm couscous.

As I climbed the companionway ladder I watched the oblique orange morning light cut through the steam rising from the bowls.

"Couscous with cashews and raisins. What a treat. Is there a name for this recipe, Chef?"

"Breakfast Couscous" I said with a smile.

We slouched into the starboard cockpit cushions and filled our bellies. I watched our island home for the last month flash by at a breathtaking seven knots per hour. Within two hours we passed Punta Tuna. Punta Tuna is a very dramatic headland that marks the bottom right corner of Puerto Rico. I felt a tinge of nostalgia as we sailed away from the beautiful coastline.

"When you see the land disappearing behind you, do you feel like you're leaving somewhere or going somewhere?" I asked Wendy.

"What do you mean?" she asked.

"When you watch the coast of Puerto Rico getting smaller, do you feel like you're leaving something behind?"

"No way. Do you have any idea what month this is? That's a stupid question. Of course you don't. David, it's the end of April. The hurricane season starts the beginning of June. Forget about looking back. You better do some looking forward. We have about 600 miles to go before we get to Grenada."

"Hurricanes? Don't worry about hurricanes" I said. "It's still early. We have plenty of time to make it to Grenada before the first hurricane of the season."

Quest for the Virgins

Continuing on our oblique course away from Puerto Rico, we reached the island's insular shelf about six miles offshore. The depth gauge blinked, beeped then displayed infinity. The sea started to develop a noticeable chop.

Wendy looked at me. "Is the party over?" she asked.

"We're over the shelf" I said. "It's just a bit of mixing."

A few more boat lengths and the surface of the sea was as flat as a pond.

"Look over there" I said pointing to the eastern corner of Puerto Rico. I think that's Roosevelt Roads."

Wendy looked at the chart. "I think you're right."

Roosevelt Roads is a former naval base on Puerto Rico's southeastern corner that occupies more than two thousand acres of the most beautiful real estate in the Caribbean. Like so many large scale military projects through the millennium, the construction of the Roosevelt Roads naval base (Rosie) seemed like a great idea from the 'get go'. President Roosevelt first fell in love with the splendor of rolling tropical hills, tropical breezes and breathtaking views of the cerulean blue Caribbean. It probably wasn't a hard sell. The Admirals came on board immediately to transform a piece of paradise into a naval playground. Caribbean real estate prices hadn't gone through the roof yet. The land for the base was acquired. While the feasibility study was shuttled around Washington, the Navy found it prudent to construct a few cottages, barracks, warehouses, a very adequate golf course, refrigerator and freezer storage for beer and steaks, and a landing strip.

The base may have stayed a private military Caribbean getaway if it were not for Adolf Hitler's profound delusions for world domination. When Nazi forces ramped up their aggressive campaigns in Europe, the American Navy took a fresh look at Rosie. Even though America was officially neutral in the European conflict, the U.S. Department of Defense and the British High Command were preparing for the possibly inevitable. Developing Roosevelt Roads as a major Caribbean naval base became a top priority. As World War II continued, the German Navy expanded their patrols throughout the Caribbean. That was enough to provoke the American bull dogs to stand up on their hind legs and get ready for a fight. It was wasn't quite enough to begin laying out the big bucks for building the huge infrastructure that would later become Roosevelt Roads.

Is it hard to imagine today that the Germans could have held all of Europe, invaded England and kept the British Isles as a prize? They may have accomplished it with more help from their Axis powers. This was precisely the concern that finally motivated the rapid construction of naval infrastructure at Roosevelt Roads. The base was built in the event that England fell to Germany. If the British capitulated to the German Empire, the British Navy planned to sail their fleet en masse to the Caribbean. Presumably the fleet would carry the Crown and English nobility as supercargo to set up a kingdom in exile among the palms. There would not be room on the ships for all

British subjects. They could visit later using their German passports.

Roosevelt Roads was designed to serve as the main port for the British fleet. The overflow of naval vessels would be scattered among safe harbors in the British and American Virgins. In 1941 the war wasn't going at all well for the British. Many believed that England would be forced to surrender. That same year the American War Department purchased and otherwise expropriated two thirds of Vieques to expand the naval operations at Roosevelt Roads which was only a few miles away. They didn't remove the entire civilian population. They left a few to open and close the gates.

Immediately after the purchase of Vieques, the Department of the Navy turned the eastern half of one of the world's most beautiful islands into a bombing range and the western end into a training ground for practicing beach assaults. For the Navy, the combination of Roosevelt Roads and Vieques was an unbelievable dream come true. For naval command officers, Rosie became one of the Caribbean's first all-inclusive, private resorts, offering a top-notch golf course, horse stables, ample equestrian trails and barbecues on the beach. There was something for everyone. The enlisted man only had a short walk to find a cold beer, comfort and companionship in the red light district that grew like weeds a few hundred feet from the base entrance.

It was a sweet ride if you happened to be in Roosevelt Roads. For the small remaining population of Vieques, their island paradise became hell. For year after year, naval planes dropped bombs on the island relentlessly

Green Beach Invasion

without regard for the civilian population or respect for
nature. The ground shook day and night as if gripped in
the aftershock of earthquakes. For more than twenty years,
the acrid smoke of exploded ordnance wafted in the air.
The once beautiful palm-lined Green Beach became
trodden by constant landing exercises. For the local
population's protection, the military enclosed their 2/3 of
the island in razor wire. Anyone found on government land
was subject to military justice. No longer could the
population and wild horses range across Vieques. The
island's fragile agrarian culture faded away. The lives of the
locals were turned upside down. As the bombs continued
to fall and thousands of boots pounded up Green Beach,
the people of Vieques fell into a miserable rough existence.
They were prisoners on an island that their ancestors had
called home for two thousand years. They became the
forgotten casualties of warfare.

The Second World War ended. Good triumphed
over evil, just not in Vieques. The U.S. Department of
Defense was not about to give up a good thing. Once the
wheels of the military industrial machine begin to roll, they
are unstoppable. The one thing that the 'war to end all
wars' gave to the world was a revolution in modern military
hardware. Give Vieques up after the war? Let it return to
nature? Forget it. There was a whole new generation of
military hardware to test. It hardly seems possible, but
military activity on Vieques became worse. The Cold War
was just beginning. America and her military industrial
complex had the perfect enemy and a war that could be
fought in secrecy. This was the beginning of air-

175

conditioned warfare. Scare the common man with spooks in the shadows and they'll gladly hand over their money to save themselves from phantoms. God pity the poor souls who protest.

Having to contend with the fresh threat posed by the Cold War, Roosevelt Roads and particularly Vieques took on even greater significance as a live weapons test laboratory. There was a whole new generation of rockets, missiles, landmines, depleted uranium tipped shells, and biologic aerosols to develop and experiment with.

Despite the transformation of the beautiful island of Vieques into a smoking crater in paradise, the population took a long time to become enraged. The war on Vieques continued unabated. Bad relations between the Navy and the people of Vieques also continued for decades until a quiet campaign of civil disobedience began to sweep the small island. The campaign to remove the military from Vieques germinated at the same time that protests in Puerto Rico for more political autonomy became popular. The timing was perfect. Puerto Ricans wanted to vote and be treated like Americans. The people of Vieques wanted the ground to stop shaking. To make matters worse, the economy of Vieques and Puerto Rico were going through one of the worst slumps in history. Divisions and rifts developed in the politics of the two islands. The always practical landed gentry wanted the military dollars to keep flowing. The revolutionaries wanted freedom and more control from Washington. This struggle and division was even greater in Vieques.

Green Beach Invasion

The once passive protests on Vieques became bitter
and much more aggressive in the 1990's. Then a tragic
event occurred which would eventually wipe out the
military presence in both Roosevelt Roads and Vieques.
David Sanes, a native of Vieques and a civilian employee of
the United States Navy, was killed by a U.S. bomb dropped
from a jet. It was a bit of bad timing for the Navy. Señor
Sanes' accidental death at the hands of the seemingly
antagonistic American military was all that was needed to
blow the lid off the pot.

The problem in Vieques became a cause célèbre.
Local protesters were joined by sympathetic groups and
prominent individuals from Puerto Rico, the United States
and around the world. A long list of notable liberals took
up the cause. It included political leaders Rubén Berríos,
Robert F. Kennedy Jr., Al Sharpton, and Jesse Jackson;
singers Danny Rivera, Willie Colón, and Ricky Martin;
actors Edward James Olmos and Jimmy Smits; boxer Félix
'Tito' Trinidad; baseball superstar Carlos Delgado; writers
Ana Lydia Vega, Giannina Braschi and Guatemala's Nobel
Prize winner Rigoberta Menchú. With heavyweights like
this opposing them, it was just two years before the Navy
packed up the circus and left town. It's hard to drop bombs
when celebrities are on the beach. Not only did the Navy
leave Vieques, they completely pulled out of Roosevelt
Roads a year later. Don't ever say that the U.S military can't
turn on a dime, especially when it's their dime. The deed for
all the U.S. Department of Defense property was handed to
the United States Fish and Wildlife Service and designated
the Vieques National Wildlife Refuge. Roosevelt Roads is

currently being administered by the Navy's Base Realignment and Closure Program Management Office. The search for a new owner continues.

After a six hour sail on one tack, we approached Green Beach. From miles out, we watched as the square west end of Vieques came into focus. A beautiful band of white sand shimmering in the noon day sun gently sloped up to a scraggy line of vegetation that was crowned by rustling palm trees. I furled in the two headsails. We sailed in with the main. Within two hundred feet of the beach, I luffed the main and ran to the bow. Our momentum carried us into fifteen feet of water where I dropped the anchor. The anchor set immediately.

The blue water looked fluorescent over the bright white sand. The brackish water of the mangrove lagoons on Puerto Rico seemed a distant memory.

"I forgot Puerto Rico faster than I thought I would" I said to Wendy.

Quest was the only boat in the anchorage. There wasn't a soul to be seen on the beach. We spent the rest of the afternoon swimming, enjoying the solitude and making our own invasion of Green Beach.

The sun slowly winked over the horizon. Just as I was thinking that the day couldn't possibly get any better, we sat in the cockpit side by side and watched the night lights of distant Puerto Rico turn the night sky aglow. The lights were so bright that they dimmed the stars.

"I bet if we had anchored here less than ten years ago, we would have been arrested by now" I said. "It's so peaceful. It's hard to imagine the number of practice invasions that this beach must have seen. Can you just imagine the hundreds of landing craft? The thousands of men scrambling over the sides and making a mad dash for the tree line? I bet there were a dozen machine gun emplacements all along that high ground giving the recruits a little taste of live fire. Look out there" I said pointing to the end of the beach. "Can't you just picture Robert Duvall in 'Apocalypse Now' crouching with bullets whizzing past his head soliloquizing with deep regret that 'Some day this war's gonna end'."

Sixteen

Live Targets

I woke at midnight and went to the cockpit. Wendy followed me groggy eyed a few minutes later.

"What happened? It was so calm when we went to bed. Did a big ship pass by?" she asked.

Quest was rolling hard.

"No. It's the ocean. Feel the wind. It could get pretty rough here tomorrow. We're going to shift to Ensenada Sombe when the sun comes up."

Green Beach is a long straight beach jutting into the Caribbean. It is a fair weather anchorage only, a beautiful road stead when you can get it.

"Go back to bed. I'll sleep out here. The berth feels a little claustrophobic right now" I said.

"I want to stay in the cockpit too. I'll get our pillows."

I wrapped myself up in a blanket and drifted along until the early morning sun began to rise to the occasion. With Wendy sound asleep on the cushions, I crept as stealthily as I could to the mast and slowly raised the main.

Live Targets

I was going to find out if I could get Quest sailing without waking Sleeping Beauty. The conditions were perfect. The gentle morning breeze was blowing offshore. I raised the main as quietly as I could. A puff of wind filled the sail with a snap. Quest drifted away from the beach. I sneaked back to the cockpit, loosened the wheel break and turned our small boat south.

Quest gained momentum until she was slicing through a deep blue sea. With the blanket over her head, Wendy hadn't stirred.

I cleared my throat. "Prepare to tack" I yelled.

She still didn't move. I reached over to tickle her. When I was about to touch her, she threw off the cover.

"Got you" she said. "I've been watching you pull up the anchor and raise the main. You're pretty good at single handing. Keep going, you're doing great. I'll just watch from now on" she said.

"Nice try, prepare to tack."

Within a few seconds we made a clean tack on a fresh heading of 90° due east.

The south coast of Vieques is a jagged twenty-five miles of deep bays interspersed with craggy capes. It is moderately free of reefs and obstructions. Keeping a close eye on the depth, we approached the shoreline as closely as was prudent. For the next two hours the rugged coastline of Vieques flew by in great detail.

"According to the GPS we're very close to Ensenada Sombe."

"Are you sure? I don't see any beach at all. How can you miss a mile of beach?" Wendy asked.

Quest for the Virgins

The beach at Ensenada Sombe (Sun Bay) is one of the most magnificent and highly rated beaches in the Caribbean. From out at sea, it is hidden from view by two headlands. The high bluffs of Cayo de Tierra on the left and Punta Negra on the right rise up like sentinels to form a pinched entrance only a thousand feet wide.

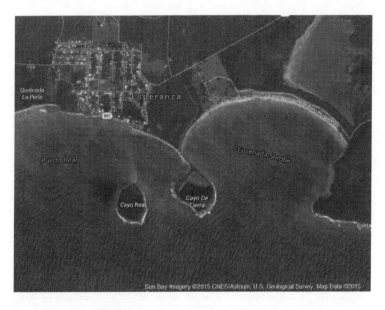

After clearing the southern tip of Cayo de Tierra we sailed into the enormous bay.

"This is unbelievable" Wendy said softly.

The immensity of the white pristine beach was impressive. An unmarred strip of sand fifty feet wide and a mile long arched in a perfect horseshoe shape. Palms and low grasses grew fifty feet from the waterline the entire length of the beach.

"Unbelievable is right" I agreed.

We anchored at the northeast corner of the anchorage in ten feet of crystal blue water. The beach was deserted and inviting.

"Let's go for a long walk on the beach" Wendy said.

"Hold on. Do you hear that?"

"This isn't going to be another 'invade the beach' joke, is it?"

"No. I think I hear some vehicles" I said.

Within seconds, two sport utility vehicles pulled up and stopped on the beach road directly in front of Quest.

"There goes the neighborhood" Wendy said.

Our first thought was that they were a couple of families coming to enjoy a day at the beach.

"Look at the gear they're pulling out of the back of that Land Cruiser" I said handing Wendy the binoculars.

"What are they going to do with all those white umbrellas?" she asked.

"Keep watching" I said.

The crew moved down to the beach and set up half a dozen tripods, then affixed the umbrellas and screwed in the lighting. They went back to the SUV and pulled out a couple of silver reflectors. The crew finished up, sat down in the high grass and lit cigarettes. Minutes later, a sparkling four door limo pulled up. Two long-legged beautiful models stepped out followed by a young man with a suitcase full of camera equipment. The photographer gave a few curt orders and the models made their way tentatively to the water's edge.

"This is definitely the right time to go for a walk" I said.

We lowered the Porta-Potty, rowed to shore and pulled the dinghy up on the sand. Looking over to the photo shoot only fifty feet away, I saw an enraged photographer starring at the Porta-Potty with disdain. He sent one of his minions to speak with us.

"Yoyo says you can't leave that horrible piece of ugly trash there."

"Horrible, ugly?" I snapped with mock anger.

"It's going to spoil the shoot" he said stepping back pleading.

"Who's Yoyo anyway?" I asked.

"He's the guy over there yelling at everybody. Look, maybe we can drag your dinghy up the beach and hide it behind that palm" he said.

"Dinghy? You mean 'Horrible Ugly' don't you?" I said with a chuckle.

"It's a very nice dinghy" he said placating me.

After pulling the Porta-Potty fifty feet up the beach I was in no mood for further direction from Yoyo. Wendy and I walked down to the waterline and began to walk up the beach.

"Stop. Stop" yelled Yoyo. "You're getting footprints all over the beach."

"Ignore him. Keep walking" I said.

Yoyo fumed, fussed, and yelled at the crew and models until we were a quarter mile up the beach. His shouts were finally muffled by the sea breeze.

"Hey, you two want a ride to town?"

We turned our heads to see a middle aged man sitting in an idling truck on the beach road.

"Sure" I said as Wendy and I climbed into the truck. "Thanks."

"I'm Jonathan. I own a hotel in town. Looks like another photo shoot on the beach. This is one of the most photographed beaches in the Caribbean. Did Yoyo and crew give you any trouble?"

"I wouldn't call it trouble. Just unfocused snarling and barking."

"I wouldn't worry about the photographers. They're harmless enough. If you stay long enough you'll see plenty of them" he laughed.

Jonathan took a right fork towards Esperanza, a small Vieques village with a beautiful name. As we drove through an upland meadow dotted with shade trees, a herd of about twenty horses ambled across the road in front of the truck.

"Who owns the horses? They seem pretty tame" Wendy asked.

"I don't know about tame. That depends on how much experience you have with handling 1000 pounds of willful beast" he said. "The Spanish brought the horses to Puerto Rico and Vieques in the 17th century. If you can understand the horses then you will understand the people of Vieques. The horses are about halfway between wild and tame. The people don't feed them, they just let them range. If the horses get into their gardens, they aren't shy about giving them a good thump with a baseball bat. Many of the locals keep saddles in their sheds. If anybody wants a horse for a couple of days for a getaway into the hills, they go find their favorite horse. As you can see, the horses aren't exactly hard to find. Sometimes if a horse takes a shine to someone it might show up at their front door. This might surprise you, but at one time Puerto Rico exported horses to the American mainland. Breeding horses was big business in the early colonial days."

We drove another mile into the center of the village.

"I'd show you around but we only have a dozen streets. You won't get lost. Come have a beer at my hotel later. It overlooks the bay" he said.

"Thanks for the ride" I said closing the door.

During our thorough twenty minute walking tour of the quiet, clean village we located a small neighborhood grocery store and a bakery. We filled our canvas shopping sack with a modest variety of tropical fruits and veggies. A few doors away we found a full scale bakery with a wide selection of breads, pastries and a few tables for walk-ins to eat breakfast. We purchased two warm baguettes, a sticky pastry and two cups of strong coffee and took a table by the window. It was only ten o'clock. The tropical heat was just starting to warm the village. Two dogs walked past the open shop door and stuck their noses in. The aged lady behind the counter picked up a broom propped against the wall and brought it down with a loud thump.

"Maldito mutts" she yelled at the dogs.

Both dogs turned and bolted up the street.

"Those dogs are worse than a couple of bad kids" she said waving the broom in the air. "They come in here every morning, sniffing around and begging."

"Why don't you just keep the door closed?" Wendy asked.

"It gets too hot in the kitchen and besides my daughter has taken to feeding those mongrels" she said sheepishly.

As we prepared to leave, I walked up to the counter.

"This bread smells great" I said holding the baguettes.

"It's good bread. I've been baking bread here for thirty years" she said with pride.

"The sweet buns are good too" Wendy said stuffing the rest in her mouth.

"Come back tomorrow. I make torpedoes on Wednesday. Good torpedoes, much lighter than the Navy used to drop on us. My torpedoes you can slice and stuff with ham and cheese" she laughed.

"It's still early. Instead of going back to Quest, let's go pay a visit to Jonathan at the hotel."

"How are we going to find it? We don't know the name of the hotel" Wendy said.

"I doubt if we'll miss it. How many hotels can there be in a twenty horse town?"

We walked down a side street towards the waterfront, crossed the beach road and stepped up on a wide promenade of red paving stones. A bright yellow concrete railing with heavy decorative balustrades ran along the cliff's edge where the promenade met the craggy drop off into the bay. We sat on a concrete bench under a trellis covered in bright red bougainvillea. It was a picture perfect panorama. Dozens of pirogues and work boats bobbed gently in the blue green surf.

"Which way to the hotel?" Wendy asked as we got up and crossed the street.

"Let's try down that way" I said turning east.

In two blocks we found ourselves standing in front of a two-story inn.

"This has to be it" I said opening the door.

A beautiful Spanish woman stepped around the counter.

"Sorry folks. The restaurant isn't open quite yet."

"No, we already had breakfast. We're looking for Jonathan" I said.

"Oh" she said looking puzzled.

"We met him on the beach this morning. He gave us a ride" I explained.

"Oh OK, he's out there" she said pointing to a set of doors.

We opened the door and found Jonathan kneeling on a canvas tarp beside a wooden kitchen chair with a paintbrush in his hand.

"Bright pink?" I said to Jonathan.

"Hola, my cruiser friends. Hey, pink is 'Vieques'. Come take a close look at this chair. Can you believe it? It's a perfectly good chair. I found it in a ditch right after I dropped you off. All it needed was a couple of coats of paint. I'm done here. Let's go have some iced tea on the upstairs porch."

We followed Jonathan through the lobby.

"Isabel, this is David and Wendy. I met them this

morning. They have a boat in Sun Bay. This is my wife Isabel" he said. "Mi amor, could you ask Angela to bring us some tea upstairs?" he said to Isabel.

"Angela's getting ready for lunch. Maybe you could get it yourself" she said looking over her glasses.

"OK, right." Turning to Wendy and me, he said "Take those stairs. I'll meet you on the veranda."

The view from the second floor was a dramatic overlook of blue sky and the Carribean as far as the eye could see.

"Pretty impressive, wouldn't you say" Jonathan mused handing me the tea. "I've owned this hotel for fifteen years. Before that, I was an Officer at Rosie. I've been around here a long time."

"Nice place to retire" Wendy said.

"I'm not quite as retiring as I thought I would be" he said with a chuckle.

"Business is good?" I asked.

"It's seasonal as you would expect. It gets busy in the winter. Not so many years ago the Navy officers had to fight for rooms. That's all changed. I haven't seen any of my old Navy buddies for years."

"What was it like here when they were dropping bombs?"

"It was bad enough. The bombing was on the east half of the island about ten miles away. The Navy completely changed the way of life on the island. To call the people of Vieques laid back is an understatement. My wife could tell you better. The Navy arrived one day and promised everyone a job and convinced them that they

189

would have a better way of life. Most people thought their lives weren't that bad. The first big change was that the Navy stopped the locals from wandering anywhere they pleased. Then the bombs started to fall. The center of the island is where the people live. It's downwind from the bombing range. Do you see how quiet it is right now? Imagine a dozen bombs going off in the next ten minutes. That can rattle your nerves. If the wind was right, the sulfur stink would roll across the village. The people are slow to anger and they are even slower to cool down. When Sanes was killed, that was it. The place started crawling with celebrities. The Navy cut their losses and moved on. They left two very big problems. Unemployment is 60% and half the people think that they are going to get cancer from the exploded ordnance."

"Is the cancer rate higher?"

"How can you tell? They smoke three packs of cigarettes a day and alcoholism is epidemic. The people of Vieques are decent people but they aren't the brightest bulbs on the string. The problem isn't whether the bombing causes cancer or the cigarettes and booze. If someone gets cancer, they are convinced that the Navy did it to them. Some people think that the Navy was testing chemicals and biologicals. You won't convince them that it isn't true. Sail down island. Go anchor in Bahia Salinas del Sur and see for yourselves. The beach and the hills are still full of old derelict jeeps and tanks that the Navy used for target practice. Just watch your step if you go to the beach. There's still plenty of un-exploded ordnance laying around. The old bombs get very touchy with age. Step on one and kaboom." He looked at his watch. "It's getting late. I need to get ready for the lunch crowd. It was great meeting you. By the way, if you talk to any of the locals, I'd suggest not bringing up the Navy. Stay and finish your tea. Enjoy yourself" he said heading for the stairs.

We thanked him for the tea, gathered up our groceries and started our walk back to Quest. A mile walk brought us to the entrance to the park reserve at Sun Bay.

"Hey, horses" Wendy said pointing to a group lounging under the shade of a breadfruit tree.

"Come on. Let's go introduce ourselves" I said.

I pulled a baguette out of the bag and left the rest of the groceries. As I approached a stallion, his ears perked up. I held out the stick of bread and walked a few feet closer. The horse started scratching the ground aggressively with his front hoof.

"See, he likes me" I said.

"Are you sure?" Wendy said.

I cautiously stepped closer. The horse came at me with an unfriendly look in his eyes.

"Run" I yelled dropping the baguette on the ground.

Both Wendy and I sprinted and dove behind a nearby breadfruit tree.

"Nice job, horse whisperer" Wendy said getting up and dusting off her pants.

We looked around the tree. The not so tame horse was casually sorting through our bag of fruit and vegetables while the rest of the herd watched on.

Seventeen

The Bay in the Bombing Zone

Living a life where physical and mental boundaries are limited only by one's concept of exploration and adventure is an ultimate expression of freedom. Wendy and I had a boat and provisions that could carry us anywhere. We arrived happily at every destination of our choosing. We were free. Wind and wave provided opportunity as well as limits. They shaped our freedom by giving it form and structure. In Quest we found refuge. With Quest we could reach out and fulfill our dreams. Within this ideal state of self-realization we had one unyielding master. Weather is God.

Our stay in Sun Bay started to feel like a vacation. Each day we awoke before dawn to watch the stars in the night sky slowly disappear and be replaced with another sparkling tropical dawn. With anticipation like children, we would row the fifty feet to shore and walk along the mile of unspoiled beach. At the end of the beach and without a care in the world we strolled side by side. Climbing the slight incline to the beach road, we walked another mile to the village. Every morning we found ourselves entering the bakery through a door left ajar for the two neighborhood dogs. A happy 'good morning' would follow our arrival. Two coffees and a pastry for Wendy would be set before us without asking. Leaving the bakery each day we walked the short distance to the grocer for a small bag of apples.

On our way back to Quest we would make a small detour to search for horses in the national reserve. In a matter of days, the horses became most friendly. They came running when we entered their sanctuary.

"I bet you never would have guessed that you would be feeding apples from Washington state to horses in Vieques" Wendy said.

"They do like the apples. They probably eat any kind of fruit."

"Do you think they eat the breadfruit from all these trees?" Wendy asked.

"These are smart horses. They don't eat breadfruit unless you make it into poi and mix it with grain" I said holding an apple at arm's length to a colt.

"Just watch your fingers."

There never seemed to be enough apples to go around. When the bag was empty, I held it up in the air then folded it ceremoniously before placing it in my back pocket and turning my back on the herd. The chestnut stallion would inevitably walk up behind me and nip at my back pocket. Before the sun was too high in the sky, we would leave the wooded horse pasture and walk to the beach with the entire herd following ten feet behind us. These idealized mornings of trips to the bakery and visits

193

with the horses were made complete by a light lunch in the cockpit, a brief nap then a swim in the warm bay. The next day we would get up and do it all over as if scripted. For Wendy and I there was happiness in routine.

These bucolic scenes in paradise would soon become snapshots, fleeting memories. Our master, the weather, had granted us only a brief shore leave. What the master gives, the master takes. The weather was about to make an abrupt change for the worse.

"There's a slow moving, sizable storm that we'll have to deal with in about four days" I said handing Wendy the fax. "Look at the wind forecast. It'll be coming straight from the south with high waves. It looks real calm now. We need to be somewhere else in a few days to weather this out" I said.

"The British Virgins?" Wendy suggested.

"Definitely not. The wind direction now is coming right from the BVI. That would be forty miles dead on the nose. I think I have a better idea. If we sail to Bahia Salina del Sur on the east end of Vieques and stay there over night, then we would have a great run to the north coast of St. Croix" I said pointing to Christiansted harbor. "Enter a course for Bahia Salina del Sur, then from Bahia Salina del Sur to Christiansted. That will keep us safe from the storm."

"Great, that will give us a whole day in the bombing range before we leave Vieques" Wendy laughed.

"There's just one more thing we need to plan for. The trip from Bahia Salina del Sur to Christiansted is about fifty miles. Averaging five knots we can count on at least a ten hour sail. Take a look at this chart. We can't take the chance of coming into Christiansted in the dark. It's littered with reefs. If we leave Bahia Salina del Sur in the early morning, say 2 AM, then we'll arrive in St. Croix a little after lunch."

"Leaving Vieques in the dark shouldn't be too bad. We're going to have a full moon tonight" Wendy added.

"The moon will help. The tough part is going to be the reefs and small islands at the entrance. When we enter the bay tomorrow, we need take a perfect set of waypoints" I said. "Better yet, run the handheld GPS at the same time that the system is gathering waypoints and verify every point."

"Don't you think that's a bit excessive?" Wendy asked.

"We have to go past these two rocks and make a hard left" I said pointing to the chart. "Sailing through this narrow at night won't be a big deal if I'm sure of our waypoints."

Without saying goodbye to the horses we hoisted the anchor and set a straight course for the bay in the center of the bombing zone. Sailing the coastline from Sun Bay to Bahia Salina del Sur is a concentrated extravaganza of deeply etched, horseshoe-shaped, brilliantly shining beaches set against a contrast of innumerable craggy headlands that reach out into the Caribbean. Like a beautiful necklace, the turquoise bays fringed by white sand beaches seem embedded in the dark rock of the headlands. They invite the sailor. Amazingly there wasn't one boat anchored anywhere on the entire coast. It was thought-provoking to imagine that there is still solitude to be had even in the over-crowded Virgins.

We began collecting waypoints on both the main GPS and the handheld as we put Alcatraz Rock to our port beam side. When this hazard was safely behind us, I made a 90° course change and steered a straight line from the rock to the northeast corner of the anchorage and set the anchor. On the chart the bay measured one mile at its widest point. It was yet another of Vieques uninhabited jewels, at least at first glance.

With the engine off, we spent a few minutes stowing all of the clutter from the day's sail. Slowly we took in the immensity of the bay. To the west on a high ridge stood a single man-made object that dominated the landscape for miles around. The tall, concrete erection appeared to be about fifty feet wide rising to a height of about one hundred feet. The most outstanding feature of the structure was that it was painted with big white and red stripes.

"What is that on top of the hill?" Wendy asked.

I handed her the binoculars.

"On the chart it's marked as an observation post. The Navy must have used it to watch the bombing. From up there you could see the entire end of the island."

At first glance the bay and wraparound hills had a natural charm if you didn't count the barber pole on top of the hill. In this case the devil was truly in the detail. We handed the binoculars back and forth. The Navy's stewardship of the east end of Vieques became more defined. Among the objects that the Navy had abandoned were a dozen bullet-ridden and bombed jeeps. Some lay half buried in sand craters just above the water line. Several lay on their sides with their tires rotting in the tropical sun. It looked like a set from an apocalypse movie. The pièce de résistance was an armored tank a few hundred feet inland that appeared in a former life to be guarding the beach. The tank's cannon barrel had been blown to bits and was pointing down at a very unnatural angle. In the few years since the naval occupation, the natural vegetation had struggled to regenerate. There was an exceptional rectangular area about 500 feet by 100 feet lying northeast of our location which had been literally bombed out of existence. Within the boundary of this concentrated bombing zone, the pockmarked ground covered in craters of various sizes was barren of all vegetation. It looked like a moonscape in miniature.

It would be amiss not to mention one example of the US Navy's more dubious actions on Vieques. What appeared as very slack behavior, the US Navy sank the USS Killen offshore a short distance from Bahia Salina del Sur. There could have been method in their madness. Scuttling a warship on the shore of a Caribbean island would seem a bit extreme in itself. The sinking of this particular warship in this particular location would seem imprudent. There are so many deep holes in the ocean in which they could have dropped the Killen. Why did they choose to leave it right in their backyard? Had the Navy grown sentimental about the Killen for some unmentioned reason? The USS Killen wasn't your normal World War Two US Navy Fletcher class destroyer. It had a very extraordinary history. Before sinking the Killen in Vieques' shallow water, it was used as a nuclear target ship in the late 1950's. Its purpose as a target ship was to determine the direct effects of radiation on a warship. An excerpt from a declassified report sponsored by the Department of Justice states that "The USS Killen was used as a target in several nuclear bomb blasts conducted in the Marshall Islands during operation HARDTACK in 1958. It was then brought back to the continental U.S. and eventually scuttled just offshore of the Atlantic Fleet Weapons Training Facility near the Live Impact Area on the eastern end of Vieques. The ship's exposure to high levels of nuclear radiation during the blast, and its current status as a local fishing and lobstering area, warranted radiological investigation of the safety of the site as well as the seafood coming from it."

The independent survey also reported some other disturbing details about Bahia Salina del Sur. Thousands of unexploded bombs were located at the bottom of the bay and surrounding hills. The study found high levels of heavy metals, TNT residue and a host of toxins in the entire area. Their recommendation was to leave the USS Killen undisturbed, remove all the visible bombs that were scattered around the beach, leave all submerged bombs *in situ* and discourage anchoring in the bay.

A great deal of thoughtful legal mediation probably took place within the upper ranks of the Navy when this over-sized problem first saw the light of day. The Navy undoubtedly cringed at the possibility of civilian scrutiny and even worse, law suits. What to do? They turned to the

The Bay in the Bombing Zone

Navy's legal counsel. A crack team of legal minds came up with the normal loophole. Donate the land to another branch of the government with the stipulation that it be maintained as a national preserve. As it turns out there is a seldom prosecuted clause that states that 'no unauthorized person or persons may cause damage to a preserve by intentionally or unintentionally disturbing the land or its vegetation'. In effect the Navy was off the hook for Vieques. If anyone ventures into the Preserve of Vieques formerly owned by the Navy and detonates a bomb by accident, they will be in violation of federal law prohibiting the destruction of a natural resource. Loopholes are so much better than trying to hide a sunk destroyer. The Navy accountants' greatest regret was that the donation wasn't tax deductible.

The more we scanned the hills and shoreline, the spookier the place became.

"Take a look at the sign on the beach" I said handing Wendy the binoculars.

"Danger Explosives. Authorized Personnel Only. No entry to Beach or Land" she read out loud.

"Hey, you want to go for a walk?" I said.

"No, I'm going to stay on the boat and rearrange my sock drawer. I'll see you if you get back" she laughed.

"I'm glad we hadn't planned on sticking around for a couple of weeks" I said.

"When you dropped the anchor, were you scared that you would hit a bomb?"

"No. There are no live bombs in this anchorage. I did look at the bottom when I dropped. All this happened ten or more years ago. I figured that if there was something down there, some poor fisherman or cruiser would have found it by now."

Bahia Salina del Sur probably isn't the first place that comes to mind when you think of paradise. On the other hand it is beautiful in its own right. The longer we looked over the picturesque Bahia Salina del Sur, the more the scene took on the appearance of one of the world's largest and strangest dioramas.

We did not go for a walk nor did we swim. We contented ourselves with sitting back with a cold beer in hand and watching the surreal shadows cast by the tangential last rays of the setting sun.

"It's about six hours before we leave" I said. "I'm going try to get some sleep."

"I'll be in shortly" Wendy said.

I went out like a light. I couldn't remember my head hitting the pillow. I woke up at midnight. After half an hour tossing and turning, I swung my legs over the side of the berth, dressed and sat in the cockpit. The moon, full, large and blue was rising in the east. It lighted the observation tower like a beacon. I watched as the moon slowly arched into a cloudless sky. I picked up the binoculars and studied the tank on the beach. The cool blue light cast by the full moon made the rusting hulk stand out in high relief. Millions of bomb craters large and small that weren't visible during the day took on great detail in the moonlight.

I swept the binoculars across the horizon. Then I saw movement at the far west corner of the bay near the scrub vegetation at the high water mark. Was it a wild horse? I refocused the binoculars. Something was definitely moving. A few moments later, a short man leading a horse by the reins appeared between two windswept trees. This seemed entirely unreal. Could that be the mythical trickster Don Genaro walking on my beach? Ambling alone in slow motion he cleared the tree line, walked down to the shore and proceeded along the beach. What would anybody be doing on this beach after midnight? The man was dressed in shorts, a sleeveless tee shirt and sandals. The horse wore a simple English saddle with no saddle bags.

Jumping down the companionway stairs I ran to the berth.

"Wendy, Wendy, you're not going to believe what's on the beach" I said excitedly.

"What's going on?" she asked.

"The cockpit, hurry." We scrambled up the companionway. "Look over there in the middle of the beach" I said.

Putting the binoculars up to her eyes she did a double take. "Unreal. This would make a great photograph for National Geographic. Take a look" she said.

As I looked through the binoculars, the lone horseman and his mount passed in and out of the angular moonlit shadows of the rusted tank, turned east and disappeared into the treeline.

Eighteen

An Island on Oil

The lone horseman walking across the moonlit bay added significant mystery and intrigue to a place abstracted from time by military adventurism. As little as seventy years ago, Bahia Salina del Sur was the quintessence of tropical beauty. The Navy tried to bomb it out of existence. In time, even the USS Killen will become just a radioactive rust spot at the bottom of the ocean.

We took one last look around the bay while the engine warmed and the mainsail was uncovered. With a bright full moon, it was the perfect night for a bit of special effects. I dropped down into the cabin and opened the navigational table. The far right back of the table was the daytime domain of the night vision scope. After every use, it was religiously returned to the same place. The night scope is a piece of space age gear that rarely sees the light of day. It was stored in a place where I could find it with my eyes closed. Returning to the cockpit, I removed the instrument from the case and turned it on. The viewfinder lit up with the familiar green phosphor glow. I pointed the scope into the inky blackness of the ocean. Every wavecrest crashing against Alcatraz Rock jumped out in brilliant streaks of saturated fluorescent green.

The anchor was raised. The Raymarine acquired the waypoints. Quest was swung around. We faced the ocean and proceeded with caution.

"Take the night scope" I said to Wendy. "Here's the trick with night scopes. Don't focus on bright shiny objects like the rock or the shore line. I can see those just fine. Focus on the subtle flashes of light green around the reefs. Remember, it's very easy to get distracted by bright shiny objects and miss all the detail. Look out there" I said pointing to Alcatraz Rock. "With this amount of moonlight, that big rock isn't much of a hazard. Look to the far left where the reefs reach out from the headland. Do you see the small flashes every time the water breaks?"

Wendy put the instrument to her eye. "I sure do."

"That's the kind of thing that you need to concentrate on. Now go to the bow and look subtle."

With waypoints enriched by Wendy's artificially enhanced visual acuity we cleared all hazards. It was time to put Bahia Salina del Sur to stern. The twenty knot cool night breeze was fresh and bracing. Off we sailed.

All classes of boats multiplied by all possible sail plans create a lot of possibilities. Where the fleet is thick and the wind and wave are mild, Quest was comparatively slow. From the deck of most boats, Quest would be perceived as a whale. But in her element she was impressive. Her fastest point of sail was very close to a close reach. Given enough wind and the right point of sail, she would take off and fly to places that lighter built boats wouldn't follow.

Wendy retired to the saloon port settee for a few hours of rest before her sunrise watch. I slouched into the cockpit cushions and covered myself with my jacket and a blanket. A feeling of well being can overtake a sailor when their boat performs beyond their expectation. It is an intimate experience. Fast sailing in favorable seas under a starry sky gives the imagination plenty of time to unwind especially in the gray zone between sleep and wakefulness. Pride in your boat and accomplishments mingle with emotion. You can be swept away during a perfect sail.

While fading in and out of consciousness under my cocoon of blanket and wind breaker, the false dawn brought deep violets and purple to the eastern horizon. I was too comfortable to get up and wake Wendy. Looking fixedly at the horizon, I tried to guess the exact spot that the sun would pop up. In that magical moment when false dawn gives way to day, the edge of the horizon flashes with a spark of warm orange. The delicate arching tip of the sun's corona peeps above the edge of the world. A sunrise is most hypnotizing at sea. I stared, entranced by the sunrise.

"What are you doing?" Wendy said from the companionway.

I looked up. Temporarily blinded by the bright sunlight, it took a few moments for my eyes to adjust.

"You were staring at the sun again."

"I guess I was" I replied.

An Island on Oil

"You're going to burn your eyeballs right out of your head some day."

"Look at the bow" I said. "Land Ho Ho. At this speed we should be off Christiansted in about three hours."

Wendy and I went forward and sat on the cabin roof underneath the billowing sails.

"What do you think of St. Croix?" I asked.

"To tell the truth, it looks pretty dry except for the little green patch at the west end."

"Let's see. On the chart, that green blob is marked as a rain forest."

"Rain forest? Hand me those binoculars" Wendy said. "Some rain forest. It looks like more like a rainless forest."

"Welcome to St. Croix. Their tourist brochure boasts that their beautiful island has the only semi-arid rain forest in the world" I said.

It wasn't long before we could see Christiansted. The top of the masts in the anchorage came into view while we were finishing a light lunch of cold chickpea, tomato and olive salad with a balsamic vinaigrette.

"Look at all those masts. That anchorage is absolutely packed" Wendy said.

"It can't be as bad as it looks" I said.

My more immediate concern was how to navigate the winding, circuitous entrance into the anchorage. A quarter of a mile from the first buoy, the sails were furled and the engine started.

"This entrance is going to be a piece of cake. Look at all these buoys. We haven't seen anything like this since

South Florida. There must be some expensive cargo that moves through here" I said.

Two 90° right turns, one 90° left turn followed by another 90° right brought us to a 200 foot wide channel between Protestant Cay and the main island. Motoring into the narrow channel, our jaws dropped. It was incomprehensible. I couldn't see us trying to eke out a space.

"There's no point even looking for a spot. Let's get out of here" I said putting the transmission in reverse a couple of times and turning Quest around. "Where are we going?" I said.

"Well, Gallows Bay is right in front of us. It says here in the cruising guide to stay out of the fairway."

"I already guessed that part. There's a spot over there."

We motored 1200 feet east and found good holding in a very storm-tossed bay. It was going to be bumpy but it was better than fighting for space by the city.

The ocean surge was pushing straight towards Quest. Before the engine was turned off, she was rocking and rolling.

"Let's take a break and go to town. Maybe the bay will calm down in a couple of hours" I said optimistically.

"I'm ready when you are" Wendy agreed.

I dropped the Porta-Potty in the heavy surf. Dinghying a short distance we pulled alongside the concrete breakwall adjacent to the marina. I tied off to a heavily rusted iron ring.

"Excuse me" I said to a marina employee in the

parking lot. "Where's the closest grocery store?"

"It's over there somewhere" he said dismissively.

"Over where?" Wendy called as he walked away.

"He's too busy" I said. "There's the restaurant. I'll ask someone in there." I approached a customer walking out the door. "Can you tell us where we can find a grocery store?"

"No, I can't" he said pushing past us.

"Friendly place" I said to Wendy.

We walked a few blocks from the marina when we saw an old black woman pushing a two wheeled cart overfilled with groceries.

"Ma'am, can you tell me where the grocery store is?"

She tightened her grip on the cart. "Over there" she said gesturing in an indeterminable direction with her head.

Standing in front of her cart, I asked a second time. "Where exactly is the store?"

Sensing an unavoidable encounter with a stranger, she pulled her cart up on the sidewalk, leaned it against a fence and secured it with a bicycle lock. "Come" she said taking hold of my tee shirt. She led me a short distance up a street, across an intersection and into the grocery store's parking lot. "Store" she said letting go of my shirt and pointing.

There wasn't much in the way of small talk on the way over. After the old woman turned to go, I looked back at Wendy. She had the 'big grin'.

"What?" I said.

"That was pretty funny. From where I was standing,

Grandma looked like she was leading her jackass up the street."

"That's about what it felt like" I said opening the door to the grocery store.

'This is a bit different' I thought walking up aisle number one. The store was a cross between an upscale gourmet shop and a liquor superstore. Twenty feet of rum bottles of every size, shape and flavor were nestling on wooden racks right across from the soft drinks section.

"Check this out Wendy. The rum is cheaper than the Pepsi."

"You think the rum is cheap. Go look at the price of beer at the back of the store."

In a back corner of the store just past the gourmet canned meat section were four full pallets of Sam Adams on sale.

"This price can't be right. Sam Adams is twice this price in Boston" I said to Wendy. "Excuse me" I said to a store clerk. "Is this the right price on the Sam Adams?"

The clerk yelled "H a r r y".

A balding, middle-aged gent came bouncing around the gourmet cookie corner. "What's the problem?" he asked me as the clerk disappeared behind a maze of gourmet cheeses.

"No problem" I said. "I just wanted to know if this was the right price on the Sam Adams."

He looked at the display. "Looks right to me. We got a boatload yesterday. Hey, if you buy ten cases I'll give you one free."

"Sounds good. There's only one problem. We don't

An Island on Oil

have a car. Can someone give us a lift back to the marina?"

"Absolutely, I'll bring you myself. Pay the cashier and I'll get the car."

Wendy snapped the credit card on the counter while I wandered about the front of the store. A moment later Harry approached and introduced a well dressed man in a sharp suit and tie.

"You're in luck. This is Nigel. He just happened to stop by." The two men looked at each other and smiled. "He'll be more than happy to give you a ride to your boat. I really have to take care of something upstairs" he said exiting.

The young man held out both hands to greet Wendy and me.

"Before I take you back to your boat, I'd like to show you something" he said with a secretive air.

We walked to the parking lot where his SUV was parked on the sidewalk in front of the store with the engine running. He opened the rear door for Wendy. A subarctic blast of icy air streamed out the door.

"My name is Nigel. I'm the top real estate agent on the island, maybe in all the Virgins. We'll pick up your beer in just a bit."

I slowly turned around, looked at Wendy and grinned. A taxi would have been a lot quicker, I thought. We started up into the hills on the east end of the island. The entire countryside was sliced and diced into neat, small subdivided lots.

Every time we passed one of Nigel's real estate signs he slowed down, pointed and announced with pride

"That's one of mine. Did I tell you that I'm the top agent in St. Croix?"

We bounced and jostled our way up a deserted, winding gravel road. When he wasn't making small talk, he was clumsily assaying our pockets.

"How far are we going?" Wendy asked.

"We're almost there. You're going to love this spot" he said smiling.

Too many minutes later we arrived at the top of a mountain. We stepped down from the vehicle onto a dirt road.

Sweeping his hand in a 360° arc, he announced "I represent this entire development. I'm the number one seller on the island."

'What development' I thought. There wasn't a house in sight.

He shepherded us to the top of the hill through thin scraggy vegetation. The view was spectacular. The turquoise sparkling Caribbean met a line of white breakers that crashed on reefs all around the island.

"I bet you've never seen the Caribbean like this before" he said with a wink.

"We don't get around much" I said deadpan.

The building lot was marked out in faded surveyor's tape and looked about an eighth of an acre.

"I've really come to like you two. I can tell that you really like the property. I'm going to make you a very special offer today because you're a real great couple." Wendy and I both suppressed a laugh. Here it comes. "Only four hundred and fifty thousand for this lot."

An Island on Oil

"Just four hundred and fifty thousand?" Wendy asked.

"Great price, eh?" This bit of blither was immediately followed by the most overused and greasiest realtor line in the book. "You know" he said with a lilting tone in his voice. "God just isn't making islands anymore."

"We're not interested" I said.

"This isn't it? Well, I've got the perfect piece of land for you two."

"How about bringing us back to the grocery store" I said.

Completely ignoring me, he got back into the SUV and we careened down the south side of the island.

"Here we go" he said pulling in front of yet another one of his signs. "I bet you're going to buy this lot in the next ten minutes" he said with self assurance.

Did he somehow have us confused with another couple who were actually interested? We stood at the edge of the lot. I picked up a rock about the size of a bowling ball and dropped it down the hill in the center of the property. The rock gained speed and tumbled down the grade at a dizzying clip taking out a foot-wide swath of vegetation.

"This lot does have a slight grade" he said. "But that's what you really want on a hill like this. It's normal in St. Croix. I have a friend that can fix it. This is a really good property. This one is only two hundred and fifty thousand. You know, God just isn't making any more islands" he said.

"What's that over there?" Wendy asked.

"Look" he said pointing in the other direction. "You can see St. John from here. It's behind those clouds over there."

"No, not St. John, that factory over there."

"Oh that, that's Hovensa" he replied.

When we were in Puerto Rico, Pierre and Laura had forewarned us that the Hovensa oil refinery dominated the southwest shore of St. Croix. At that time, the Hovensa facility was the largest refinery in the western hemisphere.

"This is the Caribbean. Where do they get crude oil?" I asked.

"I don't really know. Here and there" he said evasively.

Hovensa was a joint project between Hess Oil from Jacksonville, Florida and the Venezuelan state oil company. At precisely the same time that the US State Department was sanctioning the Venezuelan government for supporting state-organized terrorism, they were extending the other hand to close the deal of the century for the biggest oil refinery on U.S soil. We were looking at the timeless clockwork of power.

"I bet that the refinery can really stink" Wendy said.

"Absolutely not. To the contrary. It actually improves the air quality, especially downwind from the rum factory."

"We've seen enough real estate. I'm getting a bit tired. I've been up since two o'clock this morning. Maybe you could bring us back?"

"Absolutely, absolutely. I just have one more property to show you on the way back."

"Maybe some other time" Wendy said.

"How about tomorrow? I can pick you up at nine o'clock."

"Not tomorrow" we both said.

St. Croix was just not our vision of tropical paradise.

When Nigel pulled into the store's parking lot, he drove straight up on the sidewalk and left his engine running.

"Hey, I'll see you in about ten minutes. I just need to take care of a couple of things."

"What about the beer? Remember you were going to help us move the beer" I said.

"Oh yeah, that's right."

I looked a Wendy. She shrugged her shoulders.

"Never mind" I said. "We'll get a taxi."

"OK" he said closing the door and speeding away.

Harry the owner was standing just inside the door of the store when we entered.

"Sorry about that. Nigel's a real go-getter. Did he try to unload that overpriced property on top of the hill? He's been trying to sell that lot for three years. How much did he want for it, two hundred thousand?"

"I think he said one hundred thousand."

"No way. At that price, I might buy it myself and flip it. I sell a little real estate on the side."

"Here, take this" I said sliding Nigel's card into his shirt pocket.

"Well, it's getting late. Let's get that beer to your boat."

Nineteen

Loiterers and Law Breakers

When we arrived back at the dinghy dock it was obvious that my optimistic prediction for a calm Gallows Bay was completely off the mark. Harry was most gracious in helping us transport our cargo of ale from his car to the breakwall.

"I'm sure glad I don't have to sleep in Gallows Bay tonight" he said looking out at the white caps blanketing the bay.

"Sure you don't want to come out and have a cold Sam Adams?" I said.

"I don't think so. I've never been on a sailboat. Looking at your boat right now I don't think I ever will. I'm getting seasick just looking at it."

I shook Harry's hand. We dinghied back to Quest and tied off to a lee side stanchion. Quest was rolling 30° with every surge of the ocean. Maintaining a rhythm with the pitching deck, we manhandled the cases onto the boat, down the companionway and finally stowed them securely in the rear berth.

"What do you want for supper?" I asked.

"Make it light" Wendy said.

"Sam Adams and gourmet crackers" I laughed.

I opened two ice cold beers and arranged an assortment of crackers and cheese on a plate with a quarter of a pickle for effect. We sat facing the island watching the orange glow of the refinery's gas flares on the far side of the island light the night sky.

"What a long strange trip it's been: bombing zone, beer and bubbling crude" I said.

"Should we stay or should we go?" Wendy asked.

"We're not going to stay in Gallows Bay. I've been looking at the chart. Buck Island is only about an hour away. There's a very substantial reef on the northwest side. It's got to be better than this."

Five minutes after sunrise, we left it all behind. Or so I thought. Raising the anchor we motored the meandering channel to the ocean.

"There's Buck Island, baby" I said turning the helm a few degrees to starboard. "Look at that long stretch of white sand beach. Even better, look at how calm the anchorage is" I said handing Wendy the binoculars.

Wendy put the binoculars up to her eyes. "It looks almost flat. This is going to be great. Buck Island looks pretty inviting from here."

The island and particularly the extensive reefs are a jewel of nature. In 1948 the U.S. acquired Buck Island and the surrounding reefs with the goal of preserving "one of the finest marine gardens in the Caribbean Sea." The Buck Island Reef National Monument was later created by

President John F. Kennedy in 1961 and then greatly expanded in 2001 by President Bill Clinton. We were looking forward to a visit.

Even from a distance of four miles, the extensive Western Reef that reaches a mile northwest of the island was providing calm water in its lee. The approach to the island was smooth for the last quarter of a mile. The anchor was dropped a hundred feet from a pristine white sand beach that shimmered with heat in the early morning sun.

"This is more like it" Wendy said as we stored the gear.

Wendy and I were of one mind. How fast could we jump into the warm, turquoise water? We began throwing our clothes in a heap on the cockpit floor when I saw a speed boat coming from the direction of one of the nearby marinas on the island.

"You better put your clothes on quick" I said picking up the binoculars. "Wait a minute. It's a Parks boat and he's coming fast. He just turned his blue lights on."

The ranger wasn't wasting any time cutting through the whitecaps.

"What do you think he wants?" Wendy said.

"He's coming to fill the Coke machine at the nature center" I joked.

He zoomed into the anchorage and pulled up beside Quest.

"Wait a second" I said. "I'll put out some fenders."

"You don't need fenders" he said.

"Just wait until my wife ties the fenders" I said.

Loiterers and Law Breakers

When the fenders were well hung, Wendy and I reached across and took his bow and stern lines.

"She's Wendy and I'm David."

He wasn't taking names. "Let me see your permit."

"Permit, what permit?"

"Your anchoring permit."

"What permit?" I said to Wendy.

Wendy looked at me and frowned. I looked back at the ranger. We both looked at Wendy.

"We don't need a permit. It says so here in the guide." She held up the cruising guide.

"We aren't going to stay too long. Maybe just a day or two."

Wendy smiled and nodded her head yes.

"Without a permit you aren't staying here at all" he said.

"How much is the permit?" I asked.

"Fifteen dollars."

"Wendy, give the man twenty bucks."

"Wait a minute. I don't give out permits. Go to the Fort and buy a permit like everybody else. You're not staying here without a permit."

Trying to calm things down, I asked "How did you know we were out here?"

"Look over there" he said pointing to the hills on St Croix. "Do you see all those houses? I've gotten three calls on my cell phone in the last hour. There are a lot of people staring out at Buck Island. What else are they going do? If they see a boat that isn't one of their friends, they all start calling. Hey, I've got to get going. Get a permit. If I get another call I'll be back to write you a fine. Don't forget, somebody is watching you" he said self-assured.

We tossed him his lines and he crashed through waves on the way back towards the marina. Wendy looked at me.

"Don't even think about it" I said. "There's no way I'm going back and spend all day re-anchoring in Gallows Bay to buy a fifteen dollar permit."

"Are we going to stand our ground and shoot it out when he comes back?" Wendy laughed.

"No shoot outs today. We're going to raise the anchor and shoot around that reef. Then we'll shoot across to the south shore of St John's."

"I was hoping you'd say that."

"Enter the waypoints for Coral Bay."

"They're already loaded" Wendy said coyly.

Twenty minutes at Buck Island was the shortest stop we ever made. The anchor was quickly raised. It took us thirty minutes to clear the very dangerous reef on the northwest corner of the Buck Island Reef National Monument. When we cleared the modest protection that the island offered, we were into some serious wind and heavy chop. It would be a wet, wild ride to St. John's forty miles to the north.

The first settlers of St. John in the USVI were the Arawak Indians who migrated to the island from the southern Caribbean around AD 300. The more aggressive and warlike Carib Indians wiped out the Arawak in AD 1300. The Carib lived the good life for about 193 years.

Then Columbus showed up to introduce them to a more refined form of warlike aggression. With great respect and a wary eye for the politics of the Catholic church, he named the island group the Eleven Thousand Virgins in honor of the feast day of Saint Ursula and the Virgins.

Legend has it that Princess Ursula sailed from southwest Britain to join her betrothed, the pagan governor Conan Meriadoc of Armorica. Armorica was part of Gaul located between the Seine and Loire Rivers in present-day France. Before she could marry a pagan, she needed to make a pilgrimage to Rome. Legend holds that Ursula was accompanied by 11,000 virgins. While on route from Germany to Rome she was captured by Huns and the 11,000 virgins were beheaded. Historians can confirm from papal records that Ursula existed. No one believes that the lusty Huns would have killed 11,000 perfectly good virgins. The current estimate of virgins beheaded with Ursula has now been downgraded to eleven. Would Columbus have named the islands the Virgins if he had been aware that Saint Ursula's virgin head-count was off by that much?

The Virgin Islands were largely ignored by the Spanish. In a strange twist of events the British crown claimed St. John at almost the same time that the Danish government took possession in 1684. The first party of Danes that tried to settle St. John were asked to leave. The two countries disputed over ownership for a long time.

Danes can be stubborn. They persisted in their attempts to colonize St. John. In 1718 a group of twenty Danish planters and settlers from St. Thomas raised their flag at the first permanent settlement at Estate Carolina in

Coral Bay on St John. Their first interest was strategic, not agrarian. Coral Bay could protect a fleet of boats. With this tremendous harbor secured, Danish and Dutch planters established plantations on St. John. The British continued actions to reclaim the island. In 1762, to improve relations with the Danish crown, the British relinquished claims to St John. Danes are also industrious. Fifteen years later they had established 109 cotton and sugar cane plantations covering much of the island.

In the mid 1950's, the wealthy industrial magnate Laurance Rockefeller purchased most of the island of St John. His extensive land holdings were subsequently donated to the U.S. Government in 1956 to establish a National Park 'under the condition that the lands be protected from future development'. The remaining portion, the Caneel Bay Resort, operates on a lease arrangement with the National Park Service which owns the underlying land. The boundaries of the Virgin Islands National Park include 75% of the island, but various in-holdings within the park boundary (e.g. Peter Bay, Maho Bay) reduce the park lands to 60% of the island's acreage. Much of the island's waters, coral reefs and shoreline are protected by being included in the National Park. This protection was expanded in 2001 to include the newly formed Virgin Islands Coral Reef National Monument.

As we pulled away from Buck Island and started our forty mile close haul to Coral Bay, the wind began to freshen.

"Would you go below and check the VHF weather broadcast?" I said to Wendy. "This is starting to look pretty nasty."

Wendy dropped into the cabin. "Winds to twenty-five knots, seas eight to ten feet" she reported. "A small craft advisory was issued ten minutes ago. That doesn't include Quest right? She's pretty big."

"If there's a small craft advisory, it certainly does include Quest" I said. "Small craft are anything less than sixty-five feet. Don't worry about the warning. When they 'up' the advisory to 'all small craft and their crews are about to die', then give me an update."

I furled in the jib and unfurled the smaller staysail, leaving the mainsail unreefed. The sea had a considerable chop with constant blowing spray. To our good fortune the eight foot wave train was moving in our direction. The conditions only seemed worse. The ride was bumpy. Quest maintained a very even keel crossing the big waves. She answered the helm smartly. At noon there was no discussion of lunch.

We were much relieved when St John and the rest of the Virgins came into clear focus between the breaking waves. The first sight of land on a wet and bumpy trip always gives the sailor new vigor. The U.S. And British Virgins that spread out before us were breathtaking. The dark green hills that drop precipitously down to small white beaches seem to intensify the deep blues and turquoises of the ocean. This is the beauty that people seek.

As we sailed between the high headlands that define the entrance to the fjord known as Coral Bay, waves and wind were considerably reduced. There were half a dozen possible anchorages.

"The cruising guide says that Coral Harbor is a popular spot to anchor" Wendy said.

"Popular, yes. This is the Virgins. The wind is twenty five knots blowing straight from the southeast and its predicted to be 35 by tomorrow with ten foot seas. The wind will blow straight into Coral Harbor."

Looking on the chart and studying the myriad of anchorages, I found the perfect spot.

"Here you go. I like the name of this anchorage, Hurricane Hole. What more could you ask for in a hole? The far end is about two miles from the ocean. Look it up in the guide."

"It looks good. No problems" Wendy confirmed.

Coral Bay is immense. It is composed of many smaller bays. We made straight for Princess Bay in the Virgins. We entered the bay and began sounding. A few hundred feet in, the depth became uncomfortably shallow. Turning Quest around, I motored back into the main bay.

"The Princess seems a little tight" I said. "There's a promising spot I saw after we passed Otter Creek. The only problem is that the shelf drops off very fast. It's worth a try. Take the wheel and bring us in. Stop when we are in about ten feet."

"That's cutting it pretty close" Wendy said.

"The wind is hard on the nose. Just come in real slow and even if you touch bottom the wind will blow us off."

Wendy brought her in slowly.

Loiterers and Law Breakers

"Ten feet" she called.

The anchor was dropped.

"Hard reverse" I yelled.

About two hundred feet of chain should hold us. When I felt the anchor tug at the bottom, Wendy backed down hard. The rocky gravel bottom had limited holding ability. The anchor pulled right out. The third try was the charm. I went to the helm and put the engine in full reverse.

"If this doesn't yank it out of the gravel nothing will."

The anchor held. We were secure in a snug harbor with the storm worsening by the minute. When our adrenaline was back to normal, I suggested a quick dip in the crystal water before dinner. Not a boat was in sight. Our nearest neighbors occupied the houses about a half mile away on a promontory of land across the bay in the settlement of Palestina. That's far enough away I thought. I scanned the entrance two miles away. There was a boat hammering through the waves coming straight for us.

"Put your clothes back on" I said. "You're not going to believe this. There's a Parks boat coming straight for us with its blue lights on."

"Pretty funny, Dave."

It wasn't a joke. Within two minutes a carbon copy of the Buck Island patrol boat pulled alongside Quest.

An extremely straightforward ranger addressed us. "You can't stay here. This is National Park property. You have to leave by sundown."

"And go where? It's four o'clock, there's a small

223

craft advisory and a storm is coming in. Unless you want to spend the night here, I suggest you head back to the marina, Officer."

"I could ticket you" he replied.

He played his trump card too soon.

"I'm the Captain and I say it's not a good idea to go into that storm" I said.

My ace in the hurricane hole trumped his King.

"It's not that bad out there" he said softening his position.

After a minute of silence and staring, the standoff was over. He put the Parks boat in forward.

Pointing to the hills across the bay, he said "If I get one more call from the people over there, I'm coming back with the police boat."

Twenty

White Cotton, Black Slaves

"Do you think that he'll be back?" Wendy asked.

"Not unless he can find a bigger boat."

The Ranger's boat jumped from wave to wave on leaving the entrance. The gale was just beginning. Quest was tucked less than fifty feet from the shoreline in a fjord over a mile from the ocean. We were very protected from the surge but the hills of St John did practically nothing to stop the wind. The anchorage was flat. Wind howled in the rigging. The gale increased steadily for twenty four hours. There is an enormous fleet of boats in the Virgin Islands. Dire warnings were broadcast on the VHF every ten minutes. We contented ourselves with chilling in the cockpit.

The island of St John is considered the most unspoiled jewel of all the Virgin Islands. Preserving the natural beauty of St John is largely accredited to the foresight and philanthropic efforts of Laurance Rockefeller. With deep pockets and political clout, he saved St John from the land developer. The other American and British

Virgins weren't so lucky. St John is 65% natural. The rest of the Virgins have been re-engineered into developers' dreams. It is a big win for man, not for nature. Sparkling chlorinated pools, Spanish stucco facades enlivened by bougainvillea espaliers, how pretty. Nature is under the glitz and makeup.

We looked up into the tropical vegetation. It was hard to imagine that only 250 years ago, St John suffered a fate infinitely worse than the machinations of present day land sharks and pirates only twenty miles away. By 1777 the Danes were in the first phase of turning St John into a plantation island. The island is poorly suited for agriculture of any kind. The steep hills were covered in native vegetation and the soil was poor. The entire island required complete terraforming. The plantation owners had little appreciation for the natural landscape. In the spirit of enterprise, the hills were denuded of trees. Then the remaining vegetation was burned. What was left were blackened hills. The hills were too steep to grow cotton productively. They spent an inordinate amount of effort to rip the sides of the hills into terraces. There goes the neighborhood.

The seasonal planting and picking of cotton was even more laborious. The hard work was performed by field hands. The first unsuccessful plan to recruit labor was to empty the Danish prisons and bring them to St John. The prisoners turned out to be more trouble than they were worth. The owners abandoned the indentured prisoner scheme. Plan number two was to round up and enslave native Caribbean Indians. They were nearby, plentiful, docile and best of all, free for the taking. Alas, that plan went nowhere. The Indians were too frail for field work. They died by the thousands. After killing off a second generation of the plan, it was time to think big: African slaves. Importing an African workforce was very successful in the beginning. They were quite stout, had an unflagging ability to work sixteen hours in the tropical sun and responded well to whippings. They also stood up reasonably well to hot branding, starvation and torture. Almost overnight, cotton and slaves became intertwined. A whole new class of wealth in Europe was born. European ships set out in droves. Captains set the first leg of the journey to make use of favorable winds that blew them to Africa. With their human cargo tied down properly in the hold of the ship, a fast sail on the trade winds pushed them across the Atlantic straight to the Caribbean. On arrival in the New World, the confused and disoriented Africans were unloaded and the holds were quickly refilled with bales of cotton to be processed into fabric in Europe.

In the 18th century, slave trading was not a new idea. Slaving began in prehistoric times. Many scholars believe that slavery began in Africa among warring tribes with well defined social stratification. From it beginnings in Africa, the concept spread throughout all civilizations. The Danes weren't monsters. They were merciless and single minded. Unlike many other nations, they had no interest in assimilating the blacks into their society or converting them to their religious beliefs. Blacks were machines. When they broke, they were discarded. Social insanity like this couldn't survive indefinitely. After only a few years, the black population outnumbered the whites by ten to one. The Africans became restive. The year 1733 was the tipping point for black-white relations on the island.

In one single year the island of St John was ravaged by a biblical sized plague of locusts, crippled by drought and devastated by two hurricanes. The crops were destroyed and food was scarce. Conditions became so bad that slaves attempted to swim to other islands. The Danish government clamped down brutishly. Punishment became a daily exercise. It was hell in paradise. The terrified, outnumbered white population also enacted a list of punishments for those who didn't inform on fleeing slaves or for insulting a white. The stage was set for one of the worst slave revolts in history.

Interestingly, the first and only slave revolt on St John was organized by a group called the Akwamu (Akans), a tribal people from Ghana in west Africa's 'Gold Coast'. The Akwamu were a close knit group among a very diverse population of African slaves on the island of St John. In their home country of Ghana, the Akwamu traded in slaves from the vast surrounding region even before the Europeans entered the slave market. By the time that Europeans developed a market for slaves in the Americas, the supply and delivery of slaves to the Gold Coast was in African hands.

With slave trade on the increase, the Dutch, Danes, Swedes, Portuguese and British traded with the Akwamu. Ghana soon became one of the hubs for the slave trade with the Akwamu at the center. They had a healthy economy by the early 1700's. Working in the same fields beside people that they considered their inferiors must have been demeaning for the Akwamu and, as it turned out, very dangerous for the Danes.

The 1733 slave revolt of St John was organized by the Akwamu to create an Akwamu-ruled state in the Caribbean. The revolt was a clash of capitalist ideologies, not a grassroots movement to emancipate an enslaved people. The Akwamu planned a strategic capture of the island. The non-Akwamu Africans were to be kept as slaves to work the cotton plantations. One can certainly admire their vision and flare for the ironic. The Akwamu managed to capture the island in 1733. They did not loot buildings or destroy crops. For about a year they pressed their newly acquired black slaves into plantation service. There was just one problem. The reaction to the news of a renegade group of slaves going into the slave business in the Caribbean did not go over well in Europe. Warships and troops were dispatched from France and Britain to aid the Danes in recapturing St John. The revolt was suppressed. A fresh group of Danish planters resumed farming cotton.

The St. John Slave Revolt is commemorated in the Virgins on November 23rd. In 1999, the Virgin Islands legislature established November 23 as 'Virgin Island Freedom Fighters Day'. In the words of the Virgins Island government "What happened on November 23rd, 1733, if completely successful, would have marked the first independent Caribbean nation led and governed by people of African ancestry." This is absolutely true. What isn't mentioned are the Akwamu's plans of creating their own slave kingdom. The Danish abolished slavery in 1848. The cotton plantations soon went into decline. The Danish crown held the island for about twenty more years. In the early 1900's the U.S. made numerous overtures to buy St John. It wasn't until 1917 that the Danish agreed to sell the island to the U.S., fearing German expansion during World War One.

After four restful days of solitude in Hurricane Hole, the storm subsided and the clouds parted. As I weighed anchor on a sunny Sunday morning, I wondered just how many phone calls and what sort of conversations the Ranger must have had with the homeowners across the bay. We weren't sticking around to find out. Heading straight for the end of Coral Bay, we turned east into Sir Francis Drake Channel. The wind and wave were mild and steady. It was going to be a good day to sail, but exactly to where we were uncertain. We were passing into the territorial waters of the British Virgin Islands. Our final destination in the British Virgins would be the Island of Virgin Gorda. From Virgin Gorda we would sail southeast for the island of Saba in the Lesser Antilles.

The enormous charter fleet had been bottled up in port by the same storm. When we passed Road Town on Tortola, a flock of over seventy sails came billowing out of the harbor.

"Look at the fleet" I said.

The leading boat tacked to starboard. Then seventy sails tacked to starboard. For many of these bareboaters, it was their first time in the Virgins, perhaps their first time on a sailboat. What fun they were having. They had talked and planned out every day of their one week charter. They thought about it for years. It was their dream coming true. As we drew closer, we saw smiles on faces.

Within an hour, we had passed three very popular anchorages in the BVI's. Each one was three quarter filled with charter boats bobbing at their moorings. We pressed further north up Drake Channel. More charter boats appeared from every anchorage and bay. Hundreds upon hundreds of shiny boats and shiny people sailed past. Everyone sported the latest in colorful matching outerwear.

"Wow" Wendy said.

"I didn't know there were this many brand new production sailboats in the entire world. Let's head for the fuel dock in the marina at Spanish Town, buy fuel and clear Customs. Then we can blow south."

"All right" Wendy said.

We kept a wary eye trained on the boaters as we sailed straight up the center of Drake Channel. When the boat masts of the marina came into view, I picked up the VHF mic.

"Virgin Gorda Yacht Harbor, come in."

"This is the marina, over."

"This is Quest. Is there space at the fuel dock?"

"Right now there is."

"We're at the entrance. We're coming in right now."

"Go ahead."

"Can we leave the boat at the dock while we check in at Customs?"

There was a short pause. "Sure. I'll only charge you for an hour. It will be twenty-five US."

"Twenty-five bucks an hour" I said to Wendy. This is going to be expensive diesel."

"Can we skip the fuel?"

"We're going to fuel up" I said motoring to the fuel dock.

Two young men caught our lines and tied us off.

"We're going to Customs. We'll be back in twenty minutes, tops" I said placing the Baja diesel filter securely in the deck fill. "Fill the Baja slow or it will overflow" I said.

We found the Customs building up a short path from the marina. I opened the door for Wendy. A man barged right past both of us.

"I'm in a hurry" he said.

After the line jumper had cleared Customs, I walked up to the two inch thick bullet-proof glass window. I tapped the window. A rather sullen oldish black woman looked up from a romance novel.

"Don't touch the glass" she snapped.

Ouch. Trying to get on a friendlier footing I said "This is Wendy and I'm David."

I slid the passports under the glass.

"Where are you coming from and where are you going?"

"USVI and we're leaving for Saba in a couple of days. Can you check us in and out so I don't have to come back?"

She raised the Customs stamp over the passports, thump, thump. Unceremoniously she tossed the documents under the window.

"I'm giving you two days, that's it. Do you

understand?" Without waiting for a reply, she yelled "Next."

Virgin Gorda is a busy marina in the world's largest charter fleet sailing grounds. The charter industries own the waters. The few people that we met were efficiently brusque.

"Why is the Baja filter sitting in the cockpit?" I said to the dock hand when we returned.

"We're done. Didn't need the filter. Pay at the window. Hey, can you pick it up? There are two boats waiting."

It was palm trees and paradise with a big city twist. Let me out of here. After Wendy paid the bill, we cast off and sailed as fast as possible around the corner to Prickly Bay. Nosing between Mosquito Island and Virgin Gorda, we entered the bay and motored east. We stared in awe as another hundred boats sailed back and forth.

"What's that over there?" I said pointing to a patch of water void of boats and mooring balls.

"That's Robins Bay. There should be plenty of depth" Wendy said.

Robins Bay seemed like a small quiet spot in an otherwise very hectic bay devoted to boats, bars, and restaurants. Robins Bay would be our last anchorage in the Virgin Islands. It was time to leave the 'unspoiled' Virgins behind. I went below and pulled the large scale chart for the Lesser Antilles from the stack.

"Brand new" I said. "Not a single mark on the chart. This is probably the only virgin within a hundred miles."

Stepping up into the cockpit, I spread the chart on the table and we studied our future.

"What is that awful noise?" Wendy said.

We looked around to see the ferry that travels the short stretch of water between Bakers Bay to the developed area in the far east of Prickly Bay. When the boat was halfway across, the Captain abruptly changed course and veered directly at us.

"What's he doing?" Wendy said.

"He's just giving the tourists a free look around the bay."

No, it was soak the cruiser day in Virgin Gorda. We sat in the cockpit stunned as the ferry picked up speed. The captain brought the ferry within thirty-five feet of Quest then veered off in the direction of the resort. The wave slapped the hull a moment later with a crash. The cockpit was drenched.

Shaking the water off the chart, I looked at Wendy. "We'll leave for Saba tomorrow."

The End

**The Quest Series continues with
'Quest in the Caribbean'**

www.questandcrew.com

Glossary

Although you can find the nautical terms used in 'Quest for the Virgins' in your dictionary, a reader who is not a sailor may benefit from the more detailed explanations below.

AlgaeX (Chapter 10: Baja Baby) AlgaeX is a magnetic fuel conditioner that is installed in a fuel line before the primary filter in order to prevent microbial contamination of diesel fuel. Diesel fuel becomes unstable as aging, water, oxidation, and microbial contamination degrade its chemistry and quality. As fuel degrades, microscopic fuel components agglomerate forming larger clusters and organic compounds. AlgaeX technology reverses this agglomeration process. As fuel passes over the AlgaeX, its magnetic field disrupts the magnetic bond of the oxidized fuel molecules. During this disruption, the bonds are broken and the molecular clusters are reduced to their original size in the fuel. While some people think AlgaeX is snake oil, fuel specialists swear by it.

Baksheesh (Chapter 4: Proposal on the Pyramids) Baksheesh is a tip or bribe in the Middle East.

Electrolysis (Chapter 5: Fear of Falling) Electrolysis is a type of electro-chemical corrosion that can occur when two different materials connect. All compounds have electrical charges. If two different materials have different charges, then a flow of current (electrons) will occur, causing metal to erode from one of the pieces over time.

Fender (Chapter 12: Work Detail) A fender is a bumper made of inflatable rubber or plastic hung from the side of the hull to prevent damage to the boat from docks or another boat. Because they float, they can be used to mark the location of an anchor or submerged hazard.

Fiddles (Chapter 15: Invasion of Green Beach) Fiddles are movable steel bars fitted to the top of a marine stove. They are clamped around a pot so that it remains secure in a seaway.

Fuel Polishing System (Chapter 10: Baja Baby) A fuel polishing system removes contaminants like water and sludge from fuel, keeping tanks and lines clean and so preventing fuel system damage and downtime. How Quest's fuel polishing system came to be built is described in detail in 'Adrift at Sea', Chapter 6 of 'Quest on the Thorny Path'.

Gunwales (Chapter 2: Homeland insecurity) Gunwales are the top edge of the side of a boat. In old sailing ships, guns were mounted on the strong gunwales.

Halyard (Chapter 5: Fear of Falling) A halyard is a rope used for raising and lowering a sail. It is attached to the top of a sail and secured to a cleat once the sail is raised. The term comes from 'to haul yards'. Quest had four halyards running to the top of the mast – one for the main sail, one for each headsail and one for the topping lift at the end of the boom.

Heave to (Chapter 2: Homeland insecurity) Heaving to is a technique to slow and almost stop a sailboat while its sails are still up.

Insular Shelf (Chapter 15: Invasion of Green Beach) Just as a continent has a continental shelf jutting out into the ocean, an island has an insular shelf. It is a relatively shallow underwater landmass surrounding an island that extends from the waterline to the shelf break where a steep slope into greater depths begins.

Kilims (Chapter 4: Proposal on the Pyramids) Kilims are flat, handwoven, pileless tapestries made in Turkey, Iran and elsewhere in the Balkans. Lighter in weight than knotted rugs, they are used as prayer rugs, wall hangings and floor coverings.

Lifesling (Chapter 8: The Jet Ski Cometh) A Lifesling is standard Man Overboard Rescue equipment on many boats. The Lifesling is a buoyant flotation collar which is both a traditional horseshoe buoy and a helicopter rescue sling. It comes with a long length of floating line which can be used to lift a crewmember if they need help out of the water.

Luff (Chapter 2: Homeland insecurity) Luff has several meanings in sailing. When the wind over a sail is disrupted, the sail begins to flap. This flapping is called luffing because the 'luff' of the sail – its forward or leading edge – is where the flapping is most obvious. You can intentionally luff sails to slow a boat's forward motion by loosening the lines which hold the sails taut.

Masa harina (Chapter 3: On a Mission of Masa) Masa harina is a flour used in tamales and tortillas that is made from dried masa. Masa is made from dried corn soaked in a solution of lime and water which softens the corn and makes it more digestible. The limed corn is then washed and ground into dough called masa. Translated literally, masa harina means dough flour. It is not the same as corn flour or corn meal.

Mast Steps (Chapter 5: Fear of Falling) Fixed or folding mast steps allow a mast to be climbed like a giant ladder. Mast steps are made from a variety of materials. Quest was fitted with folding aluminum mast steps.

Monel (Chapter 12: Work Detail) Monel is an expensive nickel alloy that is highly resistant to corrosive conditions like seawater. It is often used as seizing wire for anchor shackles because it bends easily and will not corrode. It costs more than stainless steel.

Mossad (Chapter 4: Proposal on the Pyramids) Mossad is the Hebrew name of the Israeli national intelligence agency, also known as the Institute for Intelligence and Special Operations. It is the equivalent of the CIA in the United States.

Ortoiroid (Chapter 6: It's My Island Now) The Ortoiroid Indians were the first settlers of Puerto Rico. They are believed to have originated in the Orinoco Valley of South America, then migrated to Trinidad before proceeding further up the island chain. They were hunter gatherers who depended extensively on shellfish. In Puerto Rico, they were displaced by the Saladoid Indians.

Racor (Chapter 9: Baja Baby) Racor is a manufacturer of marine fuel filters. A Racor is usually the primary onboard filter for an engine. It removes water and solid contaminants from the fuel to protect the engine. Racor filters need to be replaced regularly, as they will clog if fuel is dirty.

Roux (Chapter 7: Bioluminescent Bay) – A roux is a

thickening agent used in sauces and soups which is usually made of equal amounts of flour and butter. Pre-cooking the roux before adding it to a sauce or soup lets the starch swell and absorb moisture, resulting in a thicker, smoother sauce.

Sail Loft (Chapter 5: Fear of Falling) A sail loft is a large open area on land used by sailmakers to spread out sails. A sailmaker's business is also called a sail loft and is often located in a true loft because so much floor space is needed to lay out sail material for inspection and sewing.

Saladoid (Chapter 6: It's My Island Now) – The Saladoid Indians were another tribe of Indians believed to have originated in Venezuela's Orinoco River who moved into the Caribbean in the 4th century BC and eventually displaced the Ortoiroid in Puerto Rico. Archaeologists believe they were the first AmerIndian potters. They survived by fishing and farming manioc.

Seizing Wire (Chapter 12: Work Detail) Seizing wire is commonly used to lock shackle pins when assembling anchor rodes. It is made of a pliable, durable, corrosion-resistant material like stainless steel or the more costly nickel alloy Monel.

Tempranillo (Chapter 3: On a Mission of Masa) Tempranillo is a full-bodied, ruby red wine native to Spain that is now grown worldwide, even in Puerto Rico.

Thorny Path (Chapter 14: Trading Winds) The thorny path is an island-hopping route to the Caribbean from south of Florida. It begins shortly after Georgetown in the southern Bahamas, proceeds south and east to the Turks and Caicos, then dips further south to Hispaniola. Mariners following the thorny path proceed east along the north coast of Hispaniola until they reach the eastern tip of the Dominican Republic. They then must cross the notoriously difficult Mona Passage to make landfall on the west coast of Puerto Rico, then follow the south coast of Puerto Rico to their destination in the Caribbean. This route appears deceptively 'thornless' and easy but mariners from Christopher Columbus to the present call it 'thorny' because it requires plowing into heavy seas against the prevailing currents and trade winds for hundreds of miles with few safe harbors for refuge. Quest and crew's trip along the thorny path can be read in 'Quest on the Thorny Path'.

TVP (Chapter 3: On a Mission of Masa, Chapter 14: Trading Winds) TVP stands for textured vegetable protein. Also known as soy meat, TVP is a soy flour product used as a meat substitute. It is sold dried in bulk or ready to eat in refrigerated packages that resemble ground meat. When hydrated, it is used to make veggie burgers, chili, spaghetti sauce, and tacos. TVP's protein content is equivalent to meat.

Yanmar (Chapter 1: Under the Radar) Yanmar is a Japanese manufacturer of marine diesel engines. Quest was equipped with a 50 horsepower naturally aspirated Yanmar engine. In 'Pirate Island', Chapter 9 of 'Quest and Crew', David describes overhauling the Yanmar engine in Fernandina Beach, Florida and the betting pool amongst the 'pirates' of the Tiger Point boatyard on whether or not the engine would start.

Yarmulke (Chapter 4: Proposal on the Pyramids) A

yarmulke is a thin skullcap or beanie worn by Jewish men to cover their head as a sign of respect for God.

Zodiac (Chapter 8: The Jet Ski Cometh) A Zodiac is a brand of inflatable boat that is often used as a sailboat's dinghy. Zodiacs are also used by lifeguards and the military.

Recipe Index

From 'Quest for the Virgins'

Vegetarian Tamales (Chapter 3: On a Mission of Masa)
Vegetarian Tamale Pie (Chapter 3: On a Mission of Masa)
Mushroom Alfredo Sauce (Chapter 7: Bioluminescent Bay)
Vegetarian Meatballs (Chapter 14: Trading Winds)
Breakfast Couscous (Chapter 15: Green Beach Invasion)

From 'Quest and Crew'

Panzone (Chapter 16: The Berries) A stove-top vegetarian calzone

From 'Quest on the Thorny Path

Stuffed Quesadilla (Chapter 7: Mayaguana)
Indian Biryani_(Chapter 13: The Sand Cay Elevator)
Fried Sosua Cheese Sandwich (Chapter 18: The Night Life)

Made in the USA
Middletown, DE
13 March 2018